PRAYER
OF POWER

PRAYER OF POWER

Written with Love by

GABRIELLA GANNON AVILA

CONFESSIONS
PUBLISHING

Prayer of Power
Copyright © 2019 by Gabriella Gannon Avila
ISBN: 978-1-7334723-2-6

Printed and bound in the United States of America.

Editors: Erick Markley & Deb Melander

Confessions Publishing is a subsidiary of Roszien Kay LLC, Lancaster, CA 93536.

For information regarding discounts on bulk purchase and all other inquiries, contact the author via email authorgabbya@gmail.com or by visiting www.prayerofpower.com

To our boys, Noah, Matthew, and Nico.

With all my love . . .

CONTENTS

INTRODUCTION

Love. "It always protects, always trusts, always hopes,
always perseveres. Love never fails . . ."

1 Corinthians 13:7-8 (NIV)

Dear Arnoldo,

I used to daydream about writing down our love story. It would be for our children and our children's children—it would be fun and beautiful and something we could read to each other when we were wrinkled and gray and wanted to remember our life together with fondness. I pictured our boys reading the story and laughing at us—at our silliness—and joking with us about all the sappy parts. Today, I have written down our love story. It is no longer just fun and beautiful. It is also painful and sorrowful. It is no longer just for our children and our children's children… it is for the world. I hope it will still bring joy and laughter and a level of silliness and jest. I also pray that it will bring hope and faith and joy to all that read our words. Our love story is about hope and joy. It is about miracles and love and what it means to hold faith in our hearts.

Friday, July 28, 2017

Dear Arnoldo,

I'm writing you this note from my heart. I have so much I want to tell you, yet so much I am afraid to say out loud. God has asked me over and over to write down all of our experiences—the journey we have been thrown into . . . but, quite frankly, I'm mad. YES, stark, raving, lunatic mad. Mad at God for allowing this, mad at life, mad, mad, mad... and sad. Sad. But ok, back to why I wrote this letter. I wrote this letter because my heart is breaking. Even now, as I'm writing, tears stream down my face. Don't get me wrong, I'm holding it together—for the boys, for my family, for your family—but then, when I'm alone... I just CAN'T. No one sees. No one knows . . . just me, just God, and now you.

When you and I are alone, I feel like it's Us—the old Us; the happy, fun-filled couple that played hooky from work to have alone-time—Us! You are my rock, my heart, MY SOUL. Now, through some sick, twisted turn of fate, here we are—in San Jose—the place of my childhood, the place of our early marriage—where we bought our first home, where our first two children came into the world... memories. Memories . . . driving, laughing together, eating, love and joy... good memories. Yet, there you are—in a hospital bed . . . and the joy disappears.

I miss you. F---, I miss you. I miss laughing with you, talking, hearing your voice... your soothing, gentle voice—the soft intonation—always hinting at fun—silly—hidden innuendos. Our secret, silly moments— you, reading my mind by catching a glimpse of my expression or finishing my sentences. You, being you. How did I find you? You fill my soul in a way that nothing can—it's like we are a part of the same candle— twin flames—that burn together. You make me laugh harder than anyone, and you somehow help me to find the beauty of who I am... My soulmate. Best Friend. Lover. Husband. Father. We really did something, you know? Our children, our marriage, our love—it is truly something incredible. It is a testament to how special you are. I could go on and on and say how you are a ridiculously hard worker, a loving father and husband—the obvious. Everyone sees this. Everyone knows this. But what I want to say is THANK YOU. Thank you for loving me, for seeing me, for showing me to love deeper than I ever thought possible. Thank you for teaching me to love myself—to trust—to believe in True Love. Thank you. I hope that in some small way, I was able to give you a small piece of joy. A small piece of love and happiness too.

This sounds like a goodbye letter. It wasn't meant to be a goodbye letter—but in some ways, I think I am saying goodbye to the old us…our old life. I'm standing on the edge of a precipice and the chasm of darkness is deep—so many unknowns. So many dreams and plans on hold— changes. I think of loss and fear. So, I hold on to God. But wait, didn't I just tell you that I am MAD at GOD? So, who do I cling to? Who's going to help me? Damn, our three boys need me so much. This keeps me going. If it were not for them—who knows what types of self-destructive things I would do. The road to the hospital is narrow and steep—it would be so easy to lose control . . . so, so easy . . .

I've never felt pain like this before. NEVER. Not even when my dad died. Parents die—that's the way of life… they get old and die. But, husbands and wives—lovers, soulmates—they venture through life together; creating life, raising them—laughing. They don't leave each other….

Seeing you in pain, in distress, is tearing me apart. You once told me: "Be strong, have faith, everything will be ok." I've clung to those words every day, and every day, I fail. But then I wake up. And every new day, I resolve to have faith and believe that somehow, after all this, our family will be ok.

God talks to me every day. I don't want to listen. I turn on the radio; I distract myself. I tell him to stop. Why? Because I'm mad—angry. But I know it's him. He tells me—he shows me—but oh, the pain hits, and I'm back to feeling scared, hurt, mad. If you could only show me a sign—a

11

true sign that it's you—my None that you are in there—that you still want to be here with me—I think it would give me strength to fight. Your silence, your unemotional resonance, your disinterest—it's killing me. I try and remember the last time you said, "Hey, beautiful." I took it for granted—I didn't know it was the last time I would hear those words. I just didn't know that this could happen to you—why you? My beautiful soul of a man... Why you?

I bargained this morning—I told God to take me—take my life for yours. To grant your full health in exchange for my life. Let's be real, you are a much better parent, provider, and person than I am—overall—not a bad bargain. But God wouldn't answer—so, I'm waiting. Then, I'm suddenly filled with faith. Like GOD is speaking to me and says, "Gabby, all you have ever wished for is happiness." That's true. I've always wished for happiness. Every birthday candle wish, for as long as I can remember—happiness, peace, joy. So, God tells me that your healing is happening and that all of this will bring us the joy and happiness we've wished for. To have FAITH. Then, I get this feeling that everything is going to be okay, and I'm filled with faith, love, hope. But I am impatient. I'm eager to hear your voice—your beautiful sing-song voice calling out, "Hey, beautiful!" as I walk down the stairs. Let it be so, God. Let it be so. And back to Faith, Strength, and Hope—I love you, Arnoldo Avila. I love you, and if one day I cannot say it—please know that you are my soul.

Love,

Your Gabby

DO YOU REMEMBER?

*"The father of a righteous child has great joy; a man
who fathers a wise son rejoices in him."*

Proverbs 23:24 (NIV)

Dear Arnoldo,

Do you remember the feeling of being totally and completely happy? Do you remember feeling carefree and filled with joy at the thought of spending a day with our boys? Do you remember when the idea of going on a short daytrip to the beach or the city filled our hearts with excitement and joy? Do you remember the pride and joy in sharing small pieces of the things we both enjoy with these little people that are so impressionable and so full of wonder and awe? That feeling of joy, of love and contentment, is what I felt on the morning of April 9, 2017.

It's so strange to think that the day that changed our lives forever began like any other ordinary Sunday. Early in the morning, as I awoke from my sleep, I heard the stomping of little feet on the wooden floor of the upstairs hallway and the giggles and chattering of Noah and Matthew, our two eldest boys. My own head was still foggy, sleepy and not wanting to wake up. I opened my eyes and saw the sun streaming through the windows, and for a moment, I panicked, forgetting that it was Sunday. It was past seven! The kids were going to be late for school, and I had to get lunches made and backpacks ready. Then the realization hit me that it was indeed Sunday, Palm Sunday to be exact—we could sleep in and relax for a bit. The door opened and I heard the footsteps of our oldest son, Noah.

"Hi Mom," he said. I knew that look.

"No electronics this early, Noah." By the look of disappointment on his face, I knew I might have a struggle.

"Here, hop in bed with us," I offered, in an effort to distract him. I made a spot for him between us. His eyes widened and he hopped in, snuggling against me. I looked over and saw you, still half-asleep, give him a wan smile. Noah snuggled in the sheets, and I hugged him.

"You know, it wasn't that long ago that you were born, and you slept right here between us…. well, it was more like you didn't sleep," I chuckled. No one slept when Noah was a baby. You looked over and gave him a pat on the head. Noah giggled and hugged you back in his sweet Noah way . . .

"Remember, Noah, what you would do when you were four years old and you wanted everyone to get up?" A mischievous smile formed, and his eyes twinkled in glee.

"I would sing . . . wake up, wake up, wake up your eyes!" he chanted. We both turned to look at you and you had your eyes closed in anticipation. We both blew air on your face and laughed. You reached over and grabbed Noah by the arm and tickled him.

"You monsters, no one ever lets me sleep around here!" you said and reluctantly got out of bed and into the shower. I stayed in bed a bit longer, basking in the warmth of a perfect morning with my boys. Contentment filled my heart. We have three gorgeous boys—Noah, our first born, was ten, Matthew was six, and Nicholas, the baby, had recently turned two years old. Our boys—our life—our world was just hours from being completely changed and here we were in this Golden moment—completely unaware. Weekends, when we have nothing to do but just BE together is my favorite thing in the whole world. Spending time with YOU and with our boys is enough. You and the boys are my world. Parenting these beautiful souls fills me with such JOY… taking in their tiny faces, their delicious baby breath, the sound of their footsteps, their laughter, the way they need us so much, and how, one day, they JUST won't need to be rocked to sleep… Their sticky hands after a park outing, the joy in their voices at your arrival after a long day of work, the joy at hearing your voice on the phone and how much they LOVE those "boys' nights out" to the Double C and Five Guys. Funny how having little people changed us—how other things stopped mattering… How you can't imagine loving anyone as much as you love them—how your life is filled with stuff and stresses, and how all of that melts away the moment you gaze at the face of your new child—still wet from birth—those eyes, tiny nose, lips so perfect they take your breath away. Ugh—those moments of happiness made me feel so much joy it hurt. Did you feel that JOY too? You must have. I know I saw that look of adoration on your face. The way those boys melted your resolve . . . I know you lived that JOY too.

This particular morning, you made the boys scrambled eggs and waffles and allowed me to take a shower in peace. You always did this. Always thought of me—always knew how hard it was to be a stay at home mom. Always thinking of others…Me… To think that this would be the last time you would stand in the kitchen making breakfast---- to think that these moments would end so abruptly . . . But we didn't know…and we lived and loved freely, basking in the unknown with full faith—full joy—fearless and strong. I want you to know that this morning was perfect. It was filled with joy and love and happiness. I want you to know that I was so happy—content and in love. I don't remember if you said, "Hey, beautiful!" as I walked down the stairs that morning. You said it so often that I took it for granted. Yes, I did. I admit that with regret. Because now, I would cut off my hand to only hear your voice say those words once again . . . to hear your voice—calling out to me... "Hey, beautiful!" So many firsts . . . and lasts. Do you remember the first time you said those words to me? I don't remember the words . . . but I remember the feeling; the way your eyes—honey-caramel eyes—locked with mine and the way our bodies connected . . . from the moment your hand touched mine—the electrical current surging through my arms. I remember my breath catching at the intensity of the feeling . . . I remember wondering if you felt it too. That feeling was our souls finding each other after millennia of being apart—that I know to be true. I know you and I are soulmates, and I know you know this too . . . So, despite the darkness that would enfold and envelope our golden world, the spark of our twin flames can never be dampened. No amount of pain, despair, or fear will ever extinguish those flames, and as I write this letter to you, I want you to know that because as strong as you are, I often wonder if you know that I know this. Be assured that I do.

With all my love...

Your sweetie,

Gabby

Dear God,

You know exactly what happened on April 9, 2017. You knew it was going to happen, you knew I would be writing you this letter, and you knew exactly what I would feel, do and think. Yet, here I am writing you this letter. More for me than for you. More for Arnoldo than for you. More for my boys than for you. Do I sound angry? Maybe a little. Do I sound scared? Yes, maybe a little too—actually, a lot. But I'm clinging to you. I have no one else. I am fully relying on you. Don't leave me. I need you.

That morning was perfect. We had an amazing breakfast and headed out on our road trip. Noah was part of a historical field trip and needed a costume. We had discovered that a woman rented costumes in Sacramento, so we decided to make a day of it. We planned to have lunch, find the costume, and walk around Old Town Sacramento. A fun family day. The type of day we loved. We piled the boys in the truck—I got into the passenger side and you drove. I looked down at my clothes—a comfy pair of jeans, tennis shoes, and a pastel-striped blouse. Comfy, but nice for a Sunday. At the last moment, I grabbed my turquoise winter jacket. April was the beginning of Spring, but the days could still be chilly. Unbeknownst to me, those clothes would accompany me during the next week. The turquoise jacket as my shelter and warmth—the tennis shoes, never once removed from my feet . . . The little details—the things you don't think about—until you do.

Sacramento is about an hour and a half from our house. The drive is beautiful. Your beautiful creations of water and earth—are always breathtaking. You know this... but I want you to know that I am grateful for them. The way the sunlight filters through the trees and dollops on the car in golden spoonfuls—the way the glistening water of the river beckons our souls—I am grateful. Grateful to see it, experience it, and take it in. The road we took involved driving along small river towns, crossing over multiple bridges, and passing scenic homes and farms. The weather was sunny but cool and crisp, and as we pulled into the city, the boys announced they were hungry. Sounded about right—growing boys eat about every two hours. We often chuckled that they would eat us out of house and home. I love to hear Arnoldo gripe about how he could never retire with the way those boys eat. It was always a tongue-in cheek quip—full of love and silliness. So, we began to look for a place to eat. I found a little café near the costume shop that I had frequented many years ago when I worked for the community college in Sacramento. I was excited to share with Arnoldo and the boys their delicious soups and sandwiches. We parked the truck and set about grabbing sippy cups, diaper bag, snacks and unloading the boys. Matthew had to use the bathroom, so I grabbed his small hand and Arnoldo grabbed baby Nico. I say "baby," but our sweet Nico was already two—toddling around in his diapers—full of life and silliness. Our Noah was old enough to follow us. The café was crowded, and we looked around for a place to sit. The only spots open were outside . . . we ordered and sat down. The boys devoured their sandwiches and I savored the soup. Arnoldo wasn't hungry. He had a few spoonfuls of my soup and drank two cups of coffee. Thinking back, that was unusual. He usually had a healthy appetite . . . but I was busy with the boys—making sure they ate—and I didn't give it much thought. Nico fussed in his highchair after having a few bites, and Arnoldo stood up to take him outside, "to let me eat," he said. I managed to have a few more sips of soup before gathering the boys to leave.

"Let's go get my costume!" Noah was impatient to leave. He crinkled his nose and scratched his dark curly hair. Both Noah and Matthew had inherited our curls and Arnoldo's big beautiful eyelashes. We walked outside to see Arnoldo and Nico playing in the corridor. The café was tucked behind a few storefronts in a quiet neighborhood. The parking area was shared by several stores. Nico grabbed Arnoldo's hand, and they walked down the hall to check out a storefront that had a broken window and glass on the ground. The broken glass was fascinating to our two-year old. The vision of Arnoldo and Nico holding hands—father and son—tiny hand in his father's big muscular one—is forever etched into my mind. Arnoldo was wearing a navy-blue pullover shirt, jeans, and loafers. He towered over Nico—his broad, muscular shoulders were gigantic next to his baby boy. Nico's golden-brown hair glistened in the light—his arm was fully stretched to capacity as he held tightly to his father's hand. He babbled on in his own language as he walked with excitement towards the broken window.

"Broken?" he looked up with wonder at his father.

"Si, esta quebrada la ventana." Arnoldo answered him in Spanish. He always felt it was so important for our boys to speak Spanish.

"Que paso?" Nico asked innocently, looking toward the broken glass and reaching down to touch it.

"Be careful," Arnoldo whispered protectively.

That scene plays over and over in my brain. The way they looked—tiny boy with his father—a toddler wondering about the scene of a broken window and his father protecting him. Superman and Superboy enjoying a moment of love and wonder.

God, you know I have felt anger and joy, humility, love, wonder, hope and hopelessness, but today, I want you to know that I also feel gratitude. Gratitude for these moments. Gratitude for the beauty in the little things of love and life.

With love and gratitude…

Your daughter,

Gabby

July 29, 2017

Dear Arnoldo,

The events that happened on April 9, 2017 will forever be a part of our love story. No matter what I do, or think, or not do—that fact cannot be changed. God has asked me to write the events down from the very first week of your accident. I don't know how; I don't know why—but I know it will all be revealed in due time. Perhaps the reason will come to you as you read these pages—maybe it will come much later—or maybe there are multiple reasons. I do know this—God wants it written, and who am I to disobey? I've avoided writing long enough. I started to write many times, but the pain in my chest came fast, the tears, the lump in my throat—it was too much when I had to be strong. Pray for me—to be strong. Thank you, Babe.

Love,

Gabby

PALM SUNDAY

"So do not fear, for I am with you; do not be dismayed, for I am your God.

I will strengthen you and help you; I will uphold
you with my righteous right hand."

Isaiah 41:10 (NIV)

od, why do I have to relive this moment? I don't want to write this. But I am doing it to be obedient to you. I'm sorry it's taken me so long. It's so very hard . . .

Sunday, April 9, 2017—Palm Sunday

We met up with our close friends, Eve and Anthony, at the costume shop. They too had a fourth-grade daughter attending the field trip who needed a costume. It was fun—Eve and her daughters joined Noah and me, and the husbands took the younger boys to the park nearby. The costume shop turned out to be in a woman's house. She had collected a large amount of period clothing and now charged a small fee for others to rent the clothing for this particular field trip. We laughed as we walked out of the dressing room. Noah looked incredibly handsome in his pioneer clothing, and since both Eve and I were planning to attend, we were required to come in the proper attire. I chose a brown pioneer dress, and Eve chose a red and black gingham. Her girls giggled as we walked out of the dressing room. Noah chose a handsome black hat to go with his pioneer outfit, and we all felt satisfied and ready to go. Arnoldo and Anthony met us outside. We had planned to have ice cream together following the shop, but Arnoldo looked tired, so I decided we should probably just head home.

"I don't feel well," he said, his brow furrowed. His skin looked slightly pale.

"What's wrong, Nonè?" I asked. Nonè was Arnoldo's family's nickname for him. It was pronounced No-nay—with the accent on the 'nay' part. His mother had called him that since he was a small child and like some things do . . . it stuck. Close family friends and family knew him by that name and that is what most called him.

"I don't know, I was changing Nico's diaper, and when I bent down to change him, I felt like I was suddenly going to throw up. Right now, I have really bad heartburn." My heart quickened.

"Heartburn?" My dad had died six years ago of a major heart attack. "Does your arm feel numb?" I asked. "Do you feel anything else?" I was already thinking of asking him to drive to the emergency room.

"No," his answer was short and annoyed. Arnoldo always hated when I would act "melodramatic" as he liked to say. He often joked that I would make a huge deal out of nothing... "It's nothing like that—just super bad heartburn."

"Maybe it was because you didn't have lunch—and drank coffee. Coffee is acidic and on an empty stomach . . ." I offered.

"Yeah, I'll just stop and get some Tums. Do you mind driving home?" Arnoldo never asked. He loved to drive—he hated to be driven. He was a fast driver and a very good one. Road trips with him at the wheel were one of his favorite pastimes. I didn't care for road trips or driving much.

I was surprised he asked. That should have been a clue to me that something was seriously wrong.

"You want me to drive?" He didn't answer. We had pulled into the Rite Aid parking lot to get his Tums. "Why don't I run inside and grab them for you. You can rest here." The kids were squabbling in the back. He was already stepping out of the truck.

"No, I'll be right back. I'll get them. I'm fine." He said and walked inside before I could answer. I've often wondered over this past year what would have happened had he stopped to talk to someone and taken a little bit longer to make his way back. What if one of the boys had asked to use the bathroom and we all had to get out of the truck? What if he had decided to grab a snack and had taken a little more time deciding? What if? What if it had all happened inside a Rite Aid—with the help of dozens of people? What if? But instead, he did exactly what he said he was going to do. He ran inside, grabbed a bottle of Tums, paid, and hurried back to the truck. Once inside, he took out three at once and chewed them fast.

"You ok?" I asked. "You still want me to drive?"

"No, I'm actually feeling better now." I handed him one more Tums, and he handed me the bottle. "I'm fine. I feel much better."

"Ok." I believed him. He headed towards the freeway. Highway 50 is the interstate that connects us to Interstate 5 and eventually back to Brentwood. He pulled onto the on-ramp, and I relaxed. My mind wandered and I looked out the window. That particular part of the freeway had no shoulder. It was an overpass, and there were small craftsman style homes twenty feet below. Traffic was slow, and as we passed, we saw a woman step outside her stopped vehicle.

"What is she doing?" Arnoldo said impatiently. He seemed frustrated.

"You don't know what might have happened," I said—not understanding the irony of that statement. "She looked like she might be in trouble." He didn't answer me, and I felt the truck accelerate around the curve of the on-ramp. I looked out the window and saw the homes. I then looked down at my phone and checked for messages. The boys were chattering in the back seat, their voices laughing and squealing in the background. I was lost in thought when I felt the truck come to a slow stop. I looked out the window and saw that we were still on the overpass. Maybe there was traffic? I looked up and saw that there were no other cars in front of us. Why had we stopped? Then, I heard it. It was a sound like nothing I had ever heard before—a low, guttural moan. I looked over and saw my husband, my lover, my soul mate, my best friend, gasping for breath. His face was a deep shade of red, and it was turned to his right side. His arms were raised over his shoulders and then suddenly slammed at an abnormally stiff posture against the steering wheel.

"What's wrong?" I screamed. "Nonè what's wrong?" He didn't answer. I looked over at the gear shifter and instinctively put the truck in park. The realization that somehow the truck was already stopped nudged my brain. I didn't have time to focus on that. His body was still shaking but the moaning was less. Somewhere in the fog, I remembered my emergency training from years prior. Always call 911 first and make sure they are on their way . . . I grabbed for a phone—and dialed 911. The woman had questions . . . "What is your emergency? Where are you? What freeway are you on? Where is the nearest exit?" I didn't know Sacramento; I wasn't paying attention to the signs as we drove—I knew we were on the freeway but wasn't sure where we were. I was losing him. We didn't have time! A police officer drove past. "Help!" I screamed, honking the horn, hoping he would stop. He kept driving. I had to do something. Arnoldo was fading fast—his face was a deep shade of crimson. I screamed and jumped out of the passenger side door and ran to Arnoldo's side. The traffic along the driver's side of the truck zoomed past us. I stepped in front of it and waved cars down. Horns blared, brakes shrieked—and I screamed and gestured for people to stop. Out of the corner of my eye, I saw a car pull over. That was all I needed. I ran over and opened his door—his body was stiffening now—barely moving—his legs were stiff—his right foot firmly pressed on the gas. I

24

could hear the truck revving up. I turned the key to turn off the truck. Nicholas, the baby, was crying; Matthew was screaming and crying, and I have no recollection of what Noah was doing. Time stood still. I unbuckled Arnoldo's safety belt and began pulling him from the car. In that moment, a woman ran up. She was short and round—I remember the way her belly pressed against her white shirt, some of the dark skin showing underneath. I felt immense peace knowing that she was there. "What happened?" she asked.

"I think he had a heart attack. I don't know—he's not breathing!" I screamed.

"I know CPR. I know CPR—let's get him on the ground." Her voice was firm and confident. I grabbed his legs and she took him under the arms, and we gently laid him on the ground. She reached inside the truck and pulled out Matthew's white jacket—and put it under his head. Immediately, she started compressions. I felt other people arrive—a man that said he was a military doctor—he worked with the woman on the compressions—another man that gently took the phone from me and spoke with the emergency personnel. I was on my knees, on the concrete, on a highway—my husband fighting for his life. From the corner of my eye, I saw a man in a dark blue jacket take flares and start putting them around the scene. Arnoldo gasped for breath, and my heart was hopeful, for a second, that he had started breathing again. She kept the compressions going—he gasped, and his face turned from a dark shade of red to purple. He stopped breathing. They felt for a pulse. There was none. I saw one single tear drop from the corner of his eye, and I knew— I knew in that moment that the love of my life was gone . . . "Don't leave me! Don't you dare leave me!" I screamed.

When the paramedics arrived, I expected them to shock him back right then and there. They didn't. They placed him on a gurney. His body was still. I screamed for them to use the paddles. Nobody listened. I was screaming against the wind and the sound of the cars. Two policemen were there. They reassured me the paramedics would use the paddles, but they had to get us off the road for our safety. They asked me if I wanted to ride in the ambulance. If I did, they would take the children in the police car, and the truck would be towed. My heart was torn between our boys and my love. Little did I know that this was the beginning of that feeling of being torn. Our family was ripped apart in seconds. I know in my heart that Arnoldo would have never wanted our boys to see or experience what they did that day. I also knew that Arnoldo would never have wanted them to be left alone. So, I chose, in that split second, to stay with them. The police officer wanted to make sure I could drive. I assured him I was fine. I got into the truck and followed him to the hospital.

I've seen movies about family rushing into the emergency room following a terrible accident—the screaming, the heightened tension are the images I remember. This was not that way. I followed the police car to the front of the hospital. It was Sunday, so there was no traffic and very few people. On the way, I called Arnoldo's brother and then our friends, Eve and Anthony. I couldn't think enough to use the truck's Bluetooth feature or to put the phone on speaker. I just called—told them the news—that I was on the way to the emergency department—that Arnoldo was hurt. Arnoldo's older brother, Mondo, was quiet and stoic on the phone. He said he would arrive shortly. Just before we hung up, he asked, "Gabby, how bad is it?"

"It's bad," I answered. There was no denying that. I couldn't avoid that truth. I knew Arnoldo had left his body on the highway that Palm Sunday afternoon. My heart had ached to stay with him . . . to make sure they kept working on him—to make sure they didn't give up on him. But I had stayed with our boys . . . our sweet innocent boys who didn't deserve any of this. There was pain like a knife in my chest.

When we arrived at the curb of the emergency department, the police officer spoke to the hospital and got permission for me to leave our truck parked there until someone could move it for us. I unloaded the boys, the diaper bag, and the stroller from the back of the truck. Nico was red in the face from crying, his cheeks hot and sweaty. Matthew and Noah were both quiet, their eyes wide, faces pale.

"Mom, what happened to Dada? Why was he making that noise?" It was Matthew asking, his sweet brown eyes clouded with fear and worry. I realized with a sinking feeling that Matthew was seated with direct line of site to his dad. He had probably seen the whole thing.

"I don't know, my love. I don't know… his heart might be sick." I answered.

"Is he going to be okay?" It was Noah asking this time. All good questions. Questions that I myself had and didn't know the answer to. I was too scared to think about that question—or to ponder it for too long. At this point, the question of whether he was alive tried to make its way into my mind. I pushed the thought out.

"I don't know, sweetie. It might take time to know that." He seemed to accept that answer.

"Mom, I don't want Matthew and Nico to not have dad. They are too young." It was Noah's quiet voice that spoke. I squeezed him tight. We walked into the emergency department behind the police officers and were quickly ushered into a private waiting room. The room had a small table and several chairs. Its walls were made of glass and were covered by linen-colored curtains. A vending machine stood in the corner.

"Do you have family coming?" one of the policemen asked.

"Yes—I called them. They are on their way here." I answered robotically. My legs felt wobbly, and I could feel my heart still pounding.

"I saw that . . . wanted to make sure you could drive—was thinking, you probably shouldn't have," he answered. I realized he was talking about me driving and talking on the cell phone while I was following him. The fact that I broke the law never crossed my mind . . . until now.

He didn't seem condescending . . .his eyes glistened with moisture and there was genuine concern.

"You ok?" he asked.

"Yes, I'll be ok," I said.

"Regardless, we are going to stick around until family arrives."

"Ok," I answered. I was numb.

"I know that's what I would want if it were my wife in your shoes," he said. "How old is he, 'bout two?" he gestured toward Nico. I nodded. "I've got a two-year-old myself." I didn't say anything—I gave him a wan smile. He cleared his throat, and they stood up and excused themselves.

"We'll be right outside if you need us," They walked out, patting Nico on the head as they walked. We were alone. Just me, Noah, Matthew and Nico—me and our boys. I gathered all the strength I could muster and knelt on my knees. I prayed and prayed and asked God for help—I dreaded the doctors walking in—I dreaded the fact that it was taking so long. Why so long? What were they not telling me? It all seemed like an eternity—but, in reality, had probably only been twenty minutes. I heard the door to the waiting room open, and I stood. A woman walked in; the policemen stepped in behind her. She had light brown hair with traces of silver; her face was plain—lines marked her forehead and mouth. She looked tired.

"Are you the wife?" she looked over to me. I nodded. "Come with me." Oh, my goodness. Come with me? That wasn't good. She wanted to talk to me outside the earshot of the boys. This couldn't be good news. The policemen motioned for me to follow her.

"Don't worry, we can watch your boys. Remember, I have one of those—" he winked as he gestured to Nico, who was banging on the vending machine. I followed the woman out of the room, trying not to think too much about our boys being left alone with complete strangers.

28

She talked as we walked. "I'm _____, the Charge Nurse today." I cannot recall her name. I probably wouldn't have been able to remember her name seconds after she said it. All I could think about was whether my husband was alive and whether I would have to now identify his body. We walked down a corridor and stood outside of a room. She pulled back a curtain and asked me to follow her. My heart was beating a thousand miles a minute, dreading what I was about to see. Would it be a sheet covering his body? The lights in the room were bright, and it was bustling with activity. Machines beeped and several people crowded around the bed. The Charge Nurse seemed impatient, "Come in," she commanded. I stepped inside. There, on a bed, was Arnoldo, his legs covered by a sheet. His chest was exposed and covered in monitors and wires. A breathing tube protruded from his mouth. His eyes were half open—I could see the whites of his eyes. His face was no longer dark crimson . . . it was back to his normal rosy complexion.

"Look honey, I want you to see this." The Charge Nurse gently gestured over to the monitor attached to his breathing tube. "You see this red light? This is him breathing on his own. We intubated him, but he's breathing over the machine. He wants to be here." I felt an immense lightness when she said this. She looked intently at my eyes as she spoke and touched my arm. "This is important—he's fighting."

"I'm here, sweetie," I said. "I'm right here—keep breathing, keep breathing." I grabbed his hand and was relieved to feel warmth. I really meant, *don't give up—I'm so proud of you.*

He wants to be here. He was breathing over the machine. Of course—that's just so Arnoldo—my Superman.

NEVER ENOUGH TIME

"Teach us to number our days that we may gain a heart of wisdom."

Psalm 90:12 (NIV)

October 1996 – Chico, CA

I remember seeing Arnoldo for the first time at a M.E.Ch.A. meeting on campus, at Chico State. M.E.Ch.A. stands for Movimiento Estudiantil Chicanos de Aztlan and is a student organization that promotes higher education, community engagement, political participation, culture, and history. I was finding myself during that time—figuring out my purpose in life and what I was meant to do. I joined several Social Justice groups—M.E.Ch.A. included. I had just started promoting free classes to help residents become U.S. citizens and had gathered volunteers. I felt empowered, young, vibrant and ready to take on the world. I had declared my major as Religious Studies when I started at Chico State, but ultimately decided I needed to also major in History, to have a full breadth of knowledge and context for both. I had no idea what I wanted to do following my undergrad studies, but I knew I needed to study what I loved. History provided me the background I needed to fuel my passion for politics, activism, and spirituality. I had a thirst for knowledge, and the education in these subjects fueled that passion.

M.E.Ch.A. meetings were always held in a small room at the bottom of the Multicultural building toward the back part of the Chico State campus. Old growth trees surrounded the old building, and I always found myself in a state of peaceful tranquility on my walk to the meetings.

I was supposed to talk in front of the group that day and discuss the Citizenship classes. As I was speaking, a new guy caught my eye. He was sitting on the couch, his hands on his hips, leaning forward. His hair was cut short—too short—military style. Ugh, not my type. I had dated a Marine in the past, and that relationship had been a disaster. He looked stiff and uncomfortable, like he didn't like being in a room full of people he didn't know. I finished my presentation and asked for volunteers. As I passed out the sign-up form, I saw that he had signed up to help for every Citizenship Class session for the semester. Years later, when we were engaged, he confessed that he had no idea what he was signing up to do. He just wanted to be with me. "I saw this gorgeous girl with long, curly hair walk in, and I knew I had to be where she was," he had said. "Man, I was mad when you didn't show up to all of the ones I went to." He thought I would be at each session, but I was the organizer and promoter for the classes and only made it to the sessions that did not have enough volunteers. I only laughed—by then, I was helplessly in love with him.

Dear Arnoldo,

Do you remember how we always felt that there was never enough time to be together? How we could spend hours and hours and hours together and never feel like it was enough? Recently I've reflected on it— on that feeling that we had always felt—like it just wasn't ever enough. The arguments we had were always about not having enough time. I'll never forget the day before my first day of school at Santa Clara University School of Law. We were laying on our bed together, in the middle of the afternoon, and you looked at me and said, "It will never be the same." You were so proud of me for getting into law school, you were so proud of me for completing and finishing—I knew then and know now that your statement wasn't meant, in any way, to discourage or take away from my accomplishments. It was simply a statement of fact, that things would change—and they did. They changed when we graduated undergrad and got full time jobs, they changed when we bought a home together, they changed when I went to law school, they changed when we had children. Change is not a bad thing—it's how we grow and learn and help others to grow and learn—but the constant in our love is our desire to be together—constantly. It always felt like we were running out of time—and maybe we were. Maybe we always knew deep down in our souls that your accident would happen. Looking back, maybe we always knew that there would be a period of time where we would be apart from each other. We wanted to savor every moment, live every second, take in every breath . . . I can proudly say . . . we did. Don't you agree? We are in unchartered waters now—living apart and trying to make sense of it all; but one thing is for sure, God is always with us. You remind me of this all the time—and I'm so grateful that you continue to be my rock, my Superman, despite it all. I love you with all my heart and soul . . .

Love,

Gabby

ALIVE

"Then the LORD God formed a man from the dust of the ground and breath into his nostrils the breath of life, and the man became a living being."

Genesis 2:7 (NIV)

April 2017

Dear God,

Arnoldo is alive! He's breathing on his own. Yes, there are tubes everywhere. Yes, they are telling me that he may not survive this—that we don't know the extent of the damage; that we don't know . . . but I do know. I know this: We have YOU, and if you are for us, who can be against us? Dearest God! Thank you for allowing him to live! For allowing him to fight!

Love,

Your Daughter

April 2017

My Dear Nonè,

I often wonder what you remember of those first hours, those first weeks that turned to months after your accident. I call it an accident because I don't know what else to call it. This letter is not just for you but also for me. Maybe writing it down will help mend the painful jagged edges and maybe healing will happen. It is meant to share the experience, from my eyes, with you—as I lived through your accident. Maybe one day, we can merge our stories together and piece them together to allow our children to know this part of our journey. Maybe. Faith. Hope. Love.

When the Charge Nurse told me that you were breathing over the machine, I felt a sense of calming power come over me. You were fighting. You wanted to live. And if there is anything I know about you, it's that once you make a decision, once you decide to do something, failure is not an option. You were fighting to live—you were fighting for you, for us, for our little family of five.

After the Charge Nurse let me see you, she ushered me out of the room because they wanted to rush you to the Cath Lab. They were going to look inside your heart to see what had caused the issue. Your brother, Mondo, had arrived, and we walked back to the small, private waiting room together. My friends Eve and Anthony had arrived as well, and Anthony spoke with the officers and left to move the truck out of the loading zone of the emergency department. The boys were tired and hungry, but all I could think about was what news the doctors had about your condition. The Cath Lab waiting area was located on a different floor of the hospital, and we were shown to the waiting room. Your sister, Angelica, arrived with her family, and our boys found themselves absorbed in play with their cousins. Little Nico went from loving arms to loving arms. My mother arrived—and more family. I was numb, high on adrenaline, tired, hungry but too scared to notice or care. After what seemed like hours, a doctor in a green gown emerged from the interior corridor. He asked to speak with me and introduced himself as a cardiologist. My heart pounded in my head. "The good news," he said calmly, "is that Arnoldo did not have a heart attack. The bad news is that we don't know what caused his heart to stop." I was unsure of what to say. I had been so sure that he had suffered a heart attack.

"What are the next steps?" I asked, my law training coming into focus and reminding me to be logical in the terror of the moment.

"Well, we are going to transfer him into the Intensive Care Unit, and they are going to run a series of tests, to see what might have caused his heart to stop, but you are all done with me and our department. Nice to have met you. Take Care." That was it. His job was done. He was the Cardiologist—it wasn't in his department—time to send Arnoldo to someone else. This was the beginning of a huge lesson for me on how the medical world works. Doctors specialize. If it isn't within their scope, they don't know, don't care, or don't want to get involved. While it makes sense logically—it takes away from the holistic view of health that, in my opinion, is essential for the best medical care for humans. Our bodily functions and organs are linked and don't stand alone. Illnesses cross over all the time—but oddly, I found that doctors did not want to cross into other fields.

Intensive Care Unit—ICU—I knew that word. I knew it wasn't good. We were asked to wait and were told that they would inform us once he was being transferred. By the time they found a room for him, the sky was dark. My friends, Eve and Rachel, offered to drive my mom and the three boys home. My brother, Jordan, was driving up from Los Angeles and would meet my mom at our home. I knelt down and wrapped the boys up in a tight hug.

"When are you and Dada coming home?" It was Matthew asking, his big brown eyes welling up in pools of tears.

"Matthew, I need you to be a big boy. Your brothers need you—I don't know when we will be home. But I need to be here to help Dada. He needs me. You will be with Ata and Uncle Jordan." Ata was my mom. Matthew perked up.

"Ok! I miss Uncle Jordan," he squealed. I gave him a kiss on the cheek. Noah was stoic, and I knew his heart was heavy.

"Be brave little man. Your dad is very proud of you. I'll be home soon. Ok?" He nodded and squeezed me tight. Nico ran up to hug me, and I squeezed him back. "I love you, baby boy," I whispered.

A male nurse approached us—a tall young guy with a buzz cut. He informed me that they were getting ready to transfer you to a room in ICU. I stood and followed. The ICU waiting area was a huge space lined with chairs along walls of windows. I followed the nurse through the waiting area to a corridor separated by two very large double steel doors. The doors made a mechanical, airy sound as they swung open and the hallway in front of us was long and wide. The walls of the hallway were bare, and the fluorescent lighting felt cold and heavy. I caught a glimpse of three nurses wheeling you into your room as I turned the corner of the hallway. The room had a large window covered by a modern shade. You were lying in bed, tubes and wires everywhere on your body. The sound of the ventilator filled the space like an ominous cloud. Two doctors stepped into the room and introduced themselves. One was the hospitalist that would be in charge of you while you were in ICU, the other indicated that he was a neurologist. I felt the acid in my stomach coming up, and I swallowed and tried to stand taller as the doctors turned to me to speak. Your brother and sister were in the room as well. We were told that you had another "seizure-like episode" as they attempted to transfer you into the room. The doctors asked me again for the story of what happened. I had already retold the story numerous times during the day, and I robotically went into a retelling of the facts. These doctors wanted to know how long it took for the ambulance to arrive. I felt my heart begin to beat faster—how long? Ten minutes, maybe fifteen? The neurologist's eyes widen.

"That is a very long time to go without oxygen," he said slowly. "How soon was CPR started?" Visions of me scrambling for the phone inside the truck while you were gasping for breath surface—I see myself screaming—running into the freeway lane and waving cars down.

"Five minutes maybe?" I'm not entirely sure of the time. It felt like an eternity. I feel the concrete pavement beneath my knees, the roar of the freeway fills my ears. The neurologist and the ICU doctor explain that they are worried about brain damage and that they would like to proceed with putting you into an induced hypothermic state. In layman's terms, they want to lower your body temp—to slow down any brain damage that may have occurred. They asked me for permission to proceed. I nodded, praying that this is the best choice for you. I didn't want to leave your side. The nurses began working on lowering your body temperature by bringing in cooling blankets and ice packets. The ICU doctor explained that they would be giving you a paralyzing medication to keep you from shivering. Shivering causes the body to heat up and they want to lower the temperature and keep it lowered. My eyes began to close, and I started fighting sleep. I curled up in the chair in your room, watching the machines work. The whirring of the cooling blanket motor lulled me into a dreamless sleep. I cannot leave your side, my Superman—my love.

Gabby

WE JUST KNEW

"For God speaks in one way, and in two, though man does not perceive it"

Job 33:14 (ESV)

Dear Arnoldo,

You and I would often retell the story of *just knowing,* in an instant, that we would spend the rest of our lives together. It was a story we both knew well and would tell each other and our children in later years.

Chico is situated about 30 miles north of the small town of Gridley. Gridley, a town known for kiwis and walnuts, was my home for the better part of my teen years and became my parent's permanent home. The drive from Chico to Gridley is on a lone stretch of highway, surrounded by open land, volcanic rock, farms and sky. It is a peaceful drive and there is no doubt that God's work is present in every landscape image. In the morning, the sun melts its golden-honey light on the open fields and hills. Radiant hues of yellow and green contrast with lavender fields. At sunset, the sky fills with red, magenta, and orange fire blazing across the sky. It radiates its beauty on the shadows of the land.

It was on one such drive back home to Gridley that I suddenly was filled with wonder at the beauty of the surrounding landscape. I began to think of you and how happy I was. By then, we had been dating just a few months. Presently, I felt an understanding enter my consciousness. It was a feeling of *knowing*—of *understanding*—and there was absolutely no doubt in my mind that you were the man I was meant to spend the rest of my life with. I knew in that moment that we were at the beginning, and that we had found each other. I was filled with peace and happiness and a strong desire to tell you about the experience!

A few days later, we met at the Blueberry Twist, a local diner in Chico and our usual homework spot. Both of us had mid-term exams looming, and the workload was beginning to add up. We sat down at a booth, ordered and began to study. I had the experience on my mind, and while I had been so anxious to tell you about it earlier in the week, I suddenly felt nervous. We had only been dating for a few months and to share something so deep and serious when we hadn't been together long was odd—yet, I couldn't shake the feeling that I needed to tell you.

"You know, on the drive home to Gridley," I began, "I started thinking about how happy we have been and, well, it's weird to say out loud but . . ." I hesitated. You had stopped writing and your gaze met mine.

"What, sweetie?"

"Well, my whole being was filled with this feeling about us . . . it's like"

"You just knew?" You finished the sentence for me.

"Yes," I whispered. "How did you know?" My hands played nervously with my pen. I doodled in the margins of my notebook.

"Because I had the exact same feeling too. I was on my drive home to San Ardo, and I just...knew. I felt weird telling you about it, so I'm glad you brought it up first." Your hands grazed mine.

"What did you just know?" I wanted you to say it—to see if you had truly felt it too.

"I just knew you were the one—the one I had been waiting for, the one I had prayed for. It's like God assured me that we were meant to be—that this is real." I was speechless for a moment. You put into words the exact feeling I felt too! It was a powerful sense of knowing that could have only come from God.

"You prayed for me?" My hand reached out to touch yours.

"Yeah," you grinned sheepishly. "I asked God for a girlfriend—but I was specific. I asked for an intelligent, beautiful girl, with long curly hair and a beautiful heart." Your hand tightened around mine. "You are all of those—beautiful inside and out, your smile lights up your face."

"I love you," I whispered. We had found each other. What's remarkable is that I too had prayed for you. I was ending an old relationship and things had not ended well. My life felt empty and meaningless. I remember being in the shower, and I cried out to God to help me find love and happiness and to help me find a man that loved and cherished me—he led me to you.

Love, Your sweetie . . .Gabby

April 1997

The front door of your apartment opens and closes. I can hear your roommate dropping his keys on the table and opening the refrigerator. I look over at you, and you are sound asleep—peaceful. It is close to 1:30 pm, and I realize that I have a class in less than 30 minutes. We had skipped morning classes to *hang out.* My bare body is covered by the soft bedspread. I move closer to you, and you wake halfway. Your head turns toward me, and you cradle my face in your hands. Your hands make their way down to the small of my back—then your lips are on my neck. I feel the intensity in your kisses, and I surrender—my afternoon classes slipping by . . .

June 1997

I'm wearing thin black pants, heels, and a white button-down blouse that flares open around my stomach. My hair cascades down my back, and I can hear your deep laughter echo downstairs. You are taking me out for drinks and dancing. It is a well-deserved break from the constant pressure of studying. Our classes have ended, and I feel light. I take one last look in the mirror and adjust my lipstick a bit before skipping down the stairs to your arms.

"Hey, beautiful!" You grab my hand and pull me in for a kiss.

"Hi, sweetie," I say . . . I have a lot on my mind, and my hand instinctively touches my navel. We head out, and you open the door to your silver pickup truck and help guide me inside. Summers in Chico are generally hot and humid, but by the evening time, the heat of the day has lessened, and a slight breeze makes the humidity more bearable. The bar and grill is located on a tree-lined street and is tucked between old brick buildings. As we walk inside, the music fills my ears, and I feel the vibration of the bass under my feet. You put your arm around my waist and pull me close. I lean into your arm and intertwine my hand around your arm, leaning my head against your shoulder. You have this way of walking when I am at your side . . . you lean into me and over me—it's almost protective and possessive. I think if it would have been anyone else, I would have been offended and annoyed, but when you do it, I can sense how you are happy to have me by your side. It's like you want to make sure that nothing changes that. At the same time, I can feel your urge to protect and pounce on anyone that might even look my way. It always made me feel at ease, anywhere I went with you—like I had my own personal super hero by my side. The bar is already full, even though the night is just beginning. We make our way to the front and order our drinks. I ask for a coke, and you look at me, surprised.

"Not drinking anything else?"

"Not really up for it tonight," I say. You nod your head and carry our drinks. There are only a few small tables scattered throughout the outer edges of the dance floor.

"You want to sit outside?" you ask. I nod my head, and we head out to the patio. Strings of lights light up a quaint patio. The summer night air is warm and the lights in the trees make shadows along the brick floor. There is a short bar with stools against the wall and a few small tables and chairs scattered along the edge. Nobody is outside, and we are alone. We choose the bar stools and sit down. I sip on my soda and look down at my hand. "Gabby, what's wrong?" you ask.

"What do you mean?" I look down at the table and don't meet your gaze.

"You've been quiet all night. I dunno—just not your usual self. Are you ok?"

I was ok. Just had a lot on my mind and I wasn't sure if I wanted to talk about it. "Look, whatever it is, we can work through it." I look up to meet your eyes. They look concerned. Your hand grasps mine. I want to tell you. I do, but I wasn't sure. I am worried and tired. I suddenly want to go home. You stay quiet . . . still observing my face.

"Look, I'm—"

"What?" You interrupt. There is an edge of impatience in your voice.

"I didn't want to say anything until I was sure—but I'm worried. I'm late."

"Late?" You look confused. Then, a wave of understanding washes over you. "You mean like your period?" Your face is pale and serene.

"Yeah, I mean, it's been almost two weeks, and my body isn't always regular, but it has been on my mind." The idea that I might be pregnant at twenty-one isn't sitting well, and I feel the urge to call it a night and go home. "I don't know... I thought we were being cautious, but what if...?

It's been on my mind, I think, and that's why I've been so quiet." Your eyes make their way to a crack in the wood on the bar. I can hear screams of laughter coming from the dance floor. My hands grip the edge of my seat. "Look, I'm only telling you because you wanted to know what was wrong. I didn't want to say anything until I was absolutely sure, but either way—I don't expect anything from you. I want you to know that. I don't want you to feel trapped or worried that I'll ask for anything. This is my mess. I just . . ." Your hands grab mine, and you stand in front of me and twirl my bar stool so that we are facing each other.

"Ssshhh . . . stop," you say. "Gabby, I meant what I said before. I JUST know I am supposed to spend the rest of my life with you. I am in this with you. We are meant to be together, and I want you to know that no matter what happens—no matter WHAT—I will not leave your side. We will face it together. I can take time off of school and work driving trucks if I need to. We will figure it out, and you will never be alone." I feel tears forming. Your eyes are fixed on mine. "I mean, what I'm saying is... no matter what happens, no matter what you decide, I am here by your side." I don't say anything. Relief washes over me. I try to smile but instead choke back a sob. You wrap your strong arms around me, and we stand there for a long time—silent, together . . .

That night, all I could think about was you—how you were willing to stand by me and face anything. I thought of our life together—a baby, how he or she would look and act . . . and instead of fear, I felt love and courage and hope. I also thought about our goals and dreams of finishing college, going to law school, traveling, and having enough money to start our life together. *What if?* I thought. What if? Two days later I had my answer.

You answered the phone on the second ring. You sounded muffled and slow like you were waking up from a nap. "Hey, babe," I said. "Remember what we talked about the other night?"

"Yeah," your voice was suddenly alert and crisp.

"It's ok . . . it was nothing." My period had arrived...two weeks late. No baby. I had been relieved... truly relieved. We were not ready for anything that serious. A part of me—a very small part of me—felt sad. It wasn't time yet . . . but I knew without a doubt that there would be a right time.

"OK." You sounded relieved too. "You ok?"

"Yes, I'm ok."

"I love you," you say. I loved you too. It was deeper than any love I had ever known.

"I love you too . . . " I whisper, wondering what the future would hold for us.

CHILD LIKE FAITH

"And he said: Truly I tell you, unless you change and become like children, you will never enter the kingdom of heaven."

Matthew 18:3 (NIV)

April 13, 2017

Anoxic Brain Injury. That was a term I had never heard before April 2017. Or maybe I had heard of it and just didn't give it much thought. After all, it hadn't been relevant to me, or us, or our life. But now, here it was. *Anoxic Brain Injury,* brain swelling, white matter. There were too many new terms—too much to process. The 24-hour hypothermic state had come and gone. Arnoldo's body had been *warmed,* and now we were told we would need to wait to see when he would awaken. An MRI was done, and I was ushered into the hallway in front of your room. The Neurologist for the ICU, Dr. H__, asked me what Arnoldo did for a living. I explained that he is a director for the biotech branch of a recruiting and consulting company.

"Is it a complex job?" he asked.

"Complex?" I wasn't sure what he meant.

"Yes," "does it require multitasking and organizational skills, etc.?" His voice was monotone, quiet, and unemotional.

"Well, yes, he runs a large team of recruiters, manages many accounts, and oversees millions of dollars' worth of contracts in the biotech industry." It felt unnatural reciting his resume.

"You need to know that he will never do that work again."

"I'm sorry . . . what?" I managed to say.

"His job sounds complicated and high functioning. His brain injury is severe, and it is doubtful that he will ever be able to go back to that type of work. I haven't read the report on his MRI, but I can tell you that being without oxygen for as long as he was, he will have many deficits."

Not be able to go back to work? He loved his work. He was so proud of his accomplishments and of coming so far. Deficits? Each word stung like a whip against my heart.

"We should know more once the MRI results come back." With that, he was gone. A quick five minutes to visit. Five minutes to tell the grieving wife that the love of her life may never be the man he once was. In my head, I heard the question: *What about God?*

It had been four days and Arnoldo had not woken up. They had frozen his body and thawed him, and now we were waiting. All the doctors had commented that the sooner a patient wakes up, the better. Every day I was hopeful. I did not leave his side. I did not change my clothes and only left his bedside to eat and use the bathroom. The striped blouse, blue jeans, sneakers, and teal coat accompanied me every day and night. Family filled the waiting room each day and night. Arnoldo's relatives from distant places came each day and waited their turn to come inside to see him. His mother and father had been on a vacation trip to Mexico and had come rushing back upon hearing the news. They now sat with me and his siblings in the hospital room, waiting for the moment that he should wake up. Yet, he was still. By now, I had gotten used to the routine of the nursing staff coming and going every twelve hours. Each shift brought a new face, ready to take on the next few hours. Respiratory therapists would come every few hours as well and check his oxygen levels and the machines. Each would comment on how he was always breathing over the machine.

When the MRI report came in, the neurologist and the ICU doctor both called me into the hallway. They were not hopeful. He had shown no signs of waking up and the imaging did not look promising. Their words were a blur . . . white matter, damage, deficits, and most likely death or no quality of life.

"It might be time to start considering ending life support." Dr. H__ was speaking. The knife in my heart was excruciating. My heart began to pound, and I felt an anger and a rage filling up my very being. End life support? He just arrived. They had just started working on him. He was breathing over the machine! WHAT ABOUT GOD? The question screamed in my head.

"End life support? It's been four days! FOUR days!" I was speaking loudly, but I didn't care. "Give him a chance to recover. He is in there—I know he is—and he is fighting to come out of this." The doctor gave me a blank look.

"Let's talk tomorrow," he suggested.

I was enraged that they would suggest an end to his life after he had fought so hard. My brothers had returned with the boys, and my mom and several close friends of our family. As I walked into the waiting room, I was immediately surrounded by well-meaning friends and family. They urged me to return home, to get a good night's rest, to take a decent shower, to eat. I hadn't eaten much all week, and I slept off and on during the night. I wasn't ready to leave. He hadn't woken up. They had suggested taking him off life support. I didn't feel as though it was safe to leave. I had to fight—fight for him. By day six, Arnoldo's youngest brother said the only words that would have ever allowed me to leave his side.

"Gabby, you need to be there for the boys. They need you too. It's what Arnoldo would want you to do. You know it. I know it. We won't leave his side and you can come back once you get some rest." He was right. My boys needed me. They were so small and so scared. I was the only parent left that could be there for them. I needed to step into Arnoldo's shoes too. I needed to be stronger than both of us when I felt that I was at my weakest.

Coming home after being at the hospital for six days felt raw and cruel. My brother Tony drove me home. Our house looked the same, it was still bright and sunny. Our yard had never looked prettier. With the warmth of spring, roses and tulips lined the walkway, and in the backyard, the climbing roses and trumpet vines had beautifully adorned the white pergola over the deck. Our neighborhood was still filled with children playing in the streets, people mowing their lawns, walking their dogs… it was all a painful reminder that life continues. Don't you know that Arnoldo's in the hospital? That he's fighting for his life? Don't you know that there are three little boys that will not get tucked into bed by their dad tonight? I wanted to shout at all of them. I swallowed my tears as we pulled into the drive. Arnoldo's black truck stood in the driveway. Just a few days earlier, we had all piled in laughing and smiling on a beautiful Sunday morning. We didn't know what was to come, and we had innocently felt that the life we had lived would go on that way forever. It was good. Too good. Arnoldo had said that once. He said, "It's like it's too good . . . like something bad is supposed to happen." I hate that he said that or even thought it. It was like he felt that he didn't deserve to live in happiness. But he did. Don't we all?

April 2017

Dear Arnoldo,

I hate that you are not home with me. Sleeping in our bed without you that first night was the worst night I have ever spent alone. I couldn't sleep. I kept waking up, and I called the Intensive Care unit every two hours to check on you. That night, I made the decision that I would not sleep on my side of the bed until you came home. I couldn't stand the empty void of your absence. Sleeping there also made me feel closer to you. I could feel your skin, your breath, your heartbeat. I was exhausted and needed rest, but sleep eluded me. I tucked in our boys that night. They asked for you. We prayed and prayed some more. They have such faith those boys. If only I could have one ounce of their faith. They know with certainty that you will be home. They are happy. Happy that I am home to tuck them in and happy with their uncles and Ata being here. They are happy to wait for you. I want you to know that. Do not worry. They are fine. They said they cannot wait until you are home too. They want you home soon. They ask when you will wake up. They want you to wake up soon.

Our friends and neighbors have started a meal train, a GoFundMe and are taking the boys to and from school. I feel Jesus all around me. They are the hands and feet of Christ. Flowers and cards adorn our kitchen, and my mom is bustling about, making food for the boys. I feel that the mothers and fathers in our little world are stepping in for us while we go through this, my love. They are here to keep our family afloat—and it's beautiful. I love you, Arnoldo. Just know your boys are fine and focus on getting better.

Love,

Gabby

HARD WORK PAYS OFF

"Whatever you do, work at it with all your heart, as working for the Lord, not for human masters." Colossians 3:23 (NIV)

Dear Noah,

One afternoon, many years ago, I was lying in bed falling asleep. I was not fully asleep—but was getting close, and when I closed my eyes, I saw a bright light and a small little hand. In that instant, I knew deep in my soul that you were coming. YOU, my sweet boy. The boy that would make me a mother and your dad a father. This dream came one week before we heard from the doctor that you were indeed a tiny little baby growing inside my belly. Noah, your birth changed your father and I so much! We had so much more to live for, and we learned quickly how to love deeper than we ever thought possible. What a gift you gave us, my son! Oh, how I wish I could take away the pain and fear of this experience. No ten-year-old boy should have to go through the pain and fear that you must be feeling. Yet, I want you to know that I am humbled in your presence. You are resilient, strong, and have such faith. I know things must be confusing and you must be missing how things used to be, but I am also getting to experience watching you grow into the man that you will become. Your father is so proud of you. I know he is. You have his sense of humor, his quick wit, his soulful eyes. Tonight, I am thinking about all the stories your father would want to tell you. There are the stories we have told you and stories we were saving for later, when you got older. I think, somehow, the story about how your dad came to ask for my hand in marriage is one that he would want you to know. It's a funny story, a sweet story, a romantic story. It is a story for all you boys, but, somehow, I think this story is one you will appreciate the most. Here goes:

Your father decided he was going to propose to me, but before he could do that, he knew he would need to ask permission from my mom and dad (your Ata and Papa Jorge). So, one afternoon, he nervously called them and asked if he could stop by after work. They said, "yes," and so he did. Of course, they had no idea that he wanted to ask to marry me and just thought he wanted to visit them. Papa Jorge wasn't home yet, and your father and Ata sat in the living room in the Gridley house making small talk. Small talk, if you don't know what that is, is when adults don't know what to say and basically talk about the weather, how work is going, and say polite things like, "How are your mom and dad?" etc. Your dad was super nervous because he was about to ask for my hand in marriage and Ata, having no idea that this was his intention, decided to ask your dad for a small favor. Now, Ata loves, loves, loves, loves to take on home improvement projects around the house. She prefers to do things herself rather than hire people to do things for her. On this particular day, Ata had recently gotten a few quotes on replacing some underground wires that brought electricity to the big outdoor pool they had. Part of the quotes included having to dig a trench that was three feet deep and fifteen feet long. Understand that each time your dad tells this story, this trench gets deeper and longer. The real size will probably forever be truly unknown.

As Ata and your dad sat uncomfortably in that living room making "small talk," a plan began to form in Ata's head, and she decided she would ask your dad to come outside and take a look at the work she was planning to do. So, they went outside, and she showed him where the pool shed and pool pump were and asked your dad if he would mind digging the trench. And so, he did. As your dad tells the story, the ground was as hard as a rock, and as he began to dig, he had to dig very hard and eventually wet the earth in order to loosen the soil. He claims he worked for many, many hours to dig that trench, and at the end of the day, he was hot, sweaty, tired and had lost his nerve to ask for my hand in marriage. He had worn his "good clothes and shoes" and they were now all full of dirt and sweat. Instead, he said goodbye and decided not to ask. A few days later, he worked up the nerve to call on them again, but this time, told them he was coming over to ask them a very important question. He did end up asking for my hand in marriage and they of course both said yes... but to this day, your father will say that he had to dig a trench to earn my hand in marriage.

As you know, your father is the hardest worker we know. He always said that you, my dear boy, could do anything . . . anything you put your mind to. He said you just need to know how to work hard to earn it. I am grateful that your dad was ready and willing to dig a fifteen-foot trench for me. He always said it was a super hard job with the best prize at the end. He's so silly half the time, but I want you to know, with all seriousness, that if that man was willing to dig a fifteen-foot trench for me, he would be willing to climb to the moon and back for you.

As you read this, he is working, working, working his way back and out of this situation. I know you know this already, but I want you to remember that on days when you feel sad or frustrated or confused that he isn't home yet. Dad is working, and through God's grace, he will succeed at coming home to you and your brothers. This I know without a doubt. I love you Noah. Dada loves you too . . . so, so much.

Love,

Mom

YOU'RE WALKING WITH ME

"Yea, though I walk through the valley of the shadow of death, I will fear no evil: for thou art with me; thy rod and thy staff they comfort me."

Psalm 23:4(KJV)

I hated being home that first weekend, and I hated that I felt that way. Our home was always our sanctuary. It is the place we chose together— "the cookie house"—as our Noah always called it. When we walked into this house, after viewing many other homes for sale, our three-year-old promptly declared that he wanted to live in the "cookie house." The homeowner had baked, and the entire house smelled like cookies. The house was dated but had "good bones." Arnoldo always laughed when I said that because he knew that "good bones" meant that a "good amount of money" would be spent fixing it up. Yet, we bought it and renovated most of the house. We picked out wood flooring, tile, new appliances, paint, molding, and we added our own touches of décor and hung up our family photos. Our boys grew up in this house. Noah was three and Matthew was three months old when we moved in. Nico was born here. This home symbolizes the warmth of our family: joy, and togetherness. Being home that first weekend, knowing Arnoldo was in the hospital, felt empty. The house was a constant reminder of the happiness we left behind. My chest ached in empty pain. My eyes burned with the tears I was constantly holding back. I forced smiles and words to leave my mouth for the children. They looked to me with faith, hope, and wonder. They were happy I was home. I am their mom. I had to be strong, even though I felt weak and scared.

That Monday morning, I returned to the hospital. He had not awakened, but he was moving. When I walked into the room, his mother, brother, and sister were there. His sister gave me a longing look of comfort, and I knew something was wrong.

"What is it?" I asked. My heart was racing.

"It started this morning," she said. "He's been shaking. The doctors think it may be because of the medication they used when they induced his coma." Arnoldo's arms were no longer limp and lifeless. His elbows were bent, and he was shaking. His teeth clenched around the breathing tube in his mouth; his body was rigid and was shaking in small, violent jerks.

"Where's the neurologist?" I asked the nurse. "Get him now." I was screaming in my head, but the words were even and calm as they escaped my mouth. A doctor walked in—it wasn't the neurologist.

"Hi, I'm Doctor G___. I'm the ICU doctor—"

"No, I need to speak to the neurologist . . ."

"Yes, he has done his rounds for the day and won't be back for some time." I felt myself shaking.

"What is happening to my husband? Why is he doing that? What is happening?"

"We think his body may be responding to the medication that was used to induce his coma when we lowered his temperature. It should be all out of his system in a day or two. In the meantime, we will watch and monitor his vitals." I turned to Arnoldo and noticed that he had begun sweating. His mother wiped his brow with a damp cloth. The doctor left the room and the nurse asked me if we needed anything. *YES, my husband back*, I screamed silently in my head. I shook my head and turned to

60

Arnoldo. His face was flushed, beads of sweat glistened on his forehead, and his arms looked stiff and unnatural, bent at the elbow across his chest. The trembling would slow down and then start again. I wanted it to stop. *Two days*, the doctor said . . . *it would get better in two days.*

By the second day, Arnoldo was not better. His heart rate was alarmingly high, and he had spiked a fever. His mother, brother, sister and I worked diligently to keep him cool. We applied cold compresses all over his body, placed damp cloths on his forehead, legs, and stomach, and kept track of the monitors. After twenty-four hours of his fever not breaking, the nurses declared that he most likely had a neurogenic fever. They explained that this meant that the brain damage had affected his body's ability to monitor his core temperature. I kept asking them how they knew this and whether it might be something else. I demanded to see the doctor and asked them to look deeper, to see if the fever might indicate something else. They ordered bloodwork and saw an elevated white blood cell count which meant Arnoldo was fighting an infection. A chest x-ray showed pneumonia. Antibiotics were ordered and his body temperature decreased. We had won a small battle, but I knew that Arnoldo was not getting the care he needed. If I had to fight and advocate for something as simple as a blood test, to determine whether or not he had an infection that might be the cause of his fever, I knew that this hospital had already given up on him.

"We need to move him," I declared to his family later that week. "We need to get him to another hospital, and it needs to happen quickly." All agreed that he was not receiving the best care at this hospital. I started the transfer process and was quickly denied. I did not realize that moving someone to another hospital would prove to be such a difficult thing. In order to move someone from one hospital to another, the hospital requesting the move would have to prove that the receiving hospital can give him a higher level of care and proving that is not easy.

I slept at the hospital and was there day and night. In between caring for Arnoldo, I walked the desolate hallways, always flooded with their eerie fluorescent lights. My brothers booked a few Airbnbs for me so that I could rest. I only used them to shower or sleep for an hour at most. Arnoldo was in critical condition and every moment counted. The strength given to me at this time was divine. Every day, I imagined myself as a warrior, putting on my armor, my shield, my boots, my sword. Every day, I came ready to battle. Arnoldo's brain began swelling, his fever came back, his heart rate increased to alarming levels, and the tremors returned in full force. Blood clots were discovered in his leg and left arm and he was placed on medication for that. The news was grim. I pushed the ICU doctors to request another transfer to a few other better equipped hospitals. All were denied. They kept saying that the level of care was the same and that a move was not only unnecessary, but possibly dangerous. I felt that God told me to keep trying. By now, prayer teams had been set up across the world for Arnoldo. Our church and the church groups with all our friends and family were praying for Arnoldo. Baptist churches, Episcopalian churches, Mormon churches. Our families in Mexico were praying, a priest that my parents knew that resided in Ireland was praying with his parish. A woman that had come to our home as an interior designer called to follow up on the purchase of our new sofa, and I shared with her our news. She prayed over the phone with me and told me that her husband was a pastor, and their entire church would begin to pray. One of Arnoldo's cousins knew the Bishop of the Arch Diocese of Monterey, and he began to pray for Arnoldo. Emails, cards, and messages began to stream in, to let me know that Arnoldo was in their prayers. I asked them to pray for him to be moved to a place that could help him.

The doctors were concerned that he had been intubated for too long and were worried about the damage the intubation was causing to his vocal cords and airway. They wanted to do a tracheotomy, but his fever continued to spike, and they discovered that he had pneumonia again. The tracheotomy could not be performed. He was placed on the same type of antibiotics as before, and I advocated for the doctors to consider giving him a different type of antibiotics. They pushed back, saying they were not necessary. I asked them to look deeper into the cause for such a high fever and the reason why the first round of antibiotics did not take care of his pneumonia. The doctors reluctantly agreed to more bloodwork. His white blood cell count was high and continued to grow, and they discovered a blood infection and possible sepsis. New antibiotics were quickly given, and Arnoldo's body fought back. Meanwhile, I roamed the hospital praying . . . pleading with God for a miracle. I asked God *why, why him?* God intervened. In our darkest hour, God was there. He had never left.

It's funny how God lets you know that he is with you. It happens in many different ways. You have to be open and recognize them, and you have to allow him in. He is always there, and he is always wanting to show us the light. Once I stopped panicking, once I stopped living in terror and fear, once I surrendered and took that first faith-filled step, my eyes were opened.

One of the first moments happened when a Catholic priest came to give Arnoldo the Sacrament of the *Anointing of the Sick*. This is an anointing of a person with holy oils and prayer by a priest. As the priest entered the room and began anointing Arnoldo, I felt a sense of familiarity and peace. He looked up and introduced himself. His face had a familiar smile, and his voice had the same peaceful resonance as a priest I knew as a child.

"Are you Father Brent? The same Father Brent that was at the Parish in Gridley and Live Oak?" I asked. It was. The priest that came to comfort my husband was the same priest that had given us God's word and comforted us every Sunday in our Sacred Heart Church in Gridley when I was a young girl. I had not seen or heard of him for over twenty-five years. He had recently been assigned to serve as Chaplain for this very hospital. *What were the odds?* He remembered our family, and we spoke about my parents and brothers. It was as if God was reminding me of the comfort of home and letting me know that everything was going to be alright. Through Father Brent, God was letting me know that he was there, right beside me, and that like a parent, he would not let me fall.

This same week I began to see Arnoldo move. It was ever so slight, but I knew that he was moving in response to my voice. Every day, the doctors would come in and shine a light in his eyes, poke at his feet and hands, and ask him to wiggle his toes. He was lifeless, and they would leave. Yet, there were moments when I was there that I would talk to him and let him know I was there, that his whole family was there, and I would ask him to move his leg if he heard me. I saw movement—ever so slight. Another time, friends from Brentwood were visiting and they were speaking to Arnoldo, and they saw his leg move in response to my voice. They also spoke to him about home, our town, me . . . One day, when I was getting ready to leave, I told Arnoldo that I would have to go home and shower soon because I hadn't showered in days, and I looked awful. My friend was in the room and said, "But you know Gabby's beautiful, no matter what." Arnoldo nodded his head and moved his arm, and we both gasped. She kept talking and asking him questions, but he didn't do it again. I told the neurologists and ICU doctors of these movements, and they said that, more than likely, they were automatic movements and not truly responding to commands. I was disappointed that they didn't believe what I was seeing, but I knew that those movements were in direct response to our questions. Over the next few days, I would ask him to move his leg if he could hear my voice, and I could see the movement—ever so slight. I had absolute hope that he was responding, despite what the doctors thought. Arnoldo was there.

The antibiotics helped control the fever and get the infection under control, but Arnoldo's extremely high heart rate, high blood pressure, and trembling movements continued. One of the ICU doctors mentioned that he felt that Arnoldo might have Paroxysmal Sympathetic Hyperactivity or "Storming." This disorder affects 15-33 percent of people with a brain injury and the symptoms include sweating, agitation, extremely high blood pressure, abnormal posturing, fevers, and more.

64

Arnoldo exhibited all of these. One doctor described it as though he was constantly in fight or flight mode—with his body in a constant state of stress. His blood pressure was increasingly high; his movements continued, and he was sweating profusely. Nothing seemed to help, and the doctors gave him an increased dosage of fentanyl and other opioids to calm him. Watching Arnoldo writhe in excruciating pain was unbearable. I kept wondering what was worse—being the person in pain or watching the love of your life in pain. I wanted to change places with him and free him from the pain. But then I thought about how Arnoldo would feel if he had to watch me go through the pain, and I came to the conclusion that watching your loved one suffer might be worse. It wasn't a choice was it? I asked God this question but didn't hear a response. I would take it, all of it—if that was God's will.

It was getting dark outside, and I had just finished talking to my boys on the phone. Arnoldo had been sedated and was not moving. The only sounds in his room were that of the ventilator and of Arnoldo coughing every 15 minutes. His pneumonia had caused a build-up of phlegm and the respiratory therapists had to come in to suction him several times in an hour. I had just gotten off the phone with a friend and neighbor who was good friends with the Chief Nursing Officer of the entire network of hospitals where Arnoldo was admitted. She assured me that her friend would work hard to make sure that Arnoldo received the best care. With that referral, several hospital administrators came in to introduce themselves; the nursing staff seemed more attentive, and overall, our requests and questions were answered promptly and swiftly. God was at work, once again. Despite the attentiveness of the nursing staff, I knew in my heart that Arnoldo would die in this hospital if we didn't move him. He was sedated and made comfortable, but they had given up. I prayed for an answer. I had reached out to our community on social media and asked for prayers for Arnoldo. Many had reached out to us and offered kind words and prayers. That night, my cell phone beeped, and I saw that someone had sent me a private message on Facebook. It was Quan, a friend I met in sixth grade, when I was eleven years old. She and I had lost touch over the years but had reconnected on social media. I had not spoken to her in person for years. What I didn't know at the time was that God had sent her as an answer to my prayers. Her message read:

Are you looking to move Arnoldo to another hospital?

I don't know how she knew that this was exactly what we needed to do, but somehow, she had seen my prayer request online and thought to reach out and ask what she could do to help. I later found out that Quan is a nurse practitioner at the hospital I wanted Arnoldo moved to, and her attending physician knew several of the admitting doctors in the Neuro-ICU. We spoke on the phone, and I explained that we had already been turned down twice. She said she would dig into the situation and find out what happened. After several days, she called me back and said that her attending physician knew the doctor that had turned us down. She had spoken to her, and the doctor agreed to speak to me *in person* about admitting Arnoldo. If I could come up with a good case for why the other hospital offered a higher level of care, she would reconsider the transfer request. Looking back, I realize that I didn't have time to prepare or think about what I would say. There was no time. My legal training came into play, and I prayed that God would lead me to the right words. When the call came in, I found a private room near the ICU waiting room. My heart was pounding as I realized that Arnoldo's life was on the line. Later, my cousin Nena dubbed this moment as *fighting the greatest case of our lives.* I remember during the years when our boys were young and I was covered in spit-up, sleep deprived, and spending my days washing bottles, doing laundry and cleaning up the never ending amount of toys in our house, I would, in frustration, ask Arnoldo, "Why in the world did I go to law school for this?" He was always so proud of my accomplishments. He always responded, "You never know, sweetie, I feel there's a strong reason for it—you just don't know it yet."

I pushed any fear I felt out of my head. As swiftly and effectively as I could, I laid out the doctors' findings on Arnoldo's case. I explained how his heart had suddenly stopped, but that there was no answer as to why, and I questioned whether further testing should be done to determine what happened. I explained his brain injury, the fact that he most likely had Paroxysmal Sympathetic Hyperactivity, and that the hospital he was in had very little knowledge of how to handle such cases. I explained that he was highly sedated because of it, but that he would most likely die if he were to remain, due to the hospital's inexperience in such cases. I argued the fact that his illness was still a mystery and that only an academic hospital would have the resources and interest in determining exactly what happened. I went on and on for a while and then stopped, waiting for her to answer. There was a brief silence on the other end. The doctor cleared her throat and said, "Have his doctor call the transfer center and resubmit the request. I will accept the request for transfer."

It was done. God had answered our prayers. Arnoldo would be moved to a different hospital. As I travel along this journey of faith with God, I have learned many things. One thing I have learned is that God speaks and works through people to answer prayers, to comfort, to communicate, and to teach. I was just starting on this path . . .and I had much to learn. To think that the sweet friend I had met in sixth grade, thirty years ago, would be the one God would use in the miracle of saving my husband Arnoldo's life is incredible. I look at the friendships our boys make each and every day in a new light. I also look at myself and wonder if I will be the answer for someone. We need to be present—to be STILL—in order to hear God's Spirit calling us.

As we prepared to transfer Arnoldo to the other hospital, I got confirmation from God that this was exactly what his plans were. I had started to have my own worries about the transfer and whether it was truly in his best interest. After all, the ICU doctors felt that the risk of transfer did not outweigh the benefit. Two days prior to his transfer, Arnoldo was supposed to have a tracheotomy. The doctor performing the surgery came in to meet me. Arnoldo's youngest brother was also in the room. Dr. F__ was a middle aged, thin woman with icy blonde hair.

Her face was pale, and she was cold and methodical as she explained the surgery and the potential risks. I listened politely and nodded along. Presently, she stopped talking and asked me if anyone had spoken to me about the other options.

"Other options?" I asked.

"Yes, well, your husband has a severe brain injury, and I believe that, in this case, it may be better for nature to take its course."

"Let nature take its course?" I wasn't getting it. Dr. F__ pressed her lips together, smiled and cleared her throat.

"Well, we can remove his breathing tube and not do a tracheotomy. It may not be something you want to do if his recovery will not happen. If he breathes on his own, then that will be great." Her eyes looked dull and lifeless. It dawned on me that she was suggesting that I let Arnoldo die. She was hinting, with a smile, that I should remove his breathing tube and allow him to suffocate. He had been in the hospital for ONLY 10 days. Without a doubt, the doctors at this hospital had all given up. They didn't see Arnoldo—*the man, a husband, brother, son, father, my soul mate*— they saw a pile of dying flesh and bones.

Looking back, I wish I would have had the courage to scream at the woman, to tell her to leave the room. Wasn't she a doctor? Wasn't there an oath? I didn't say anything. I watched her lips smile and talk and nod and politely shook my head. I was in shock and disbelief, and my brain tried to figure out a way that maybe I had misunderstood her implications. I knew in my heart what she really meant. I demanded that they not do the surgery. Arnoldo was not going to be put under the knife by doctors that were not willing to save his life. God had helped move a mountain by getting him out of this hospital.

LETTERS BETWEEN SOULMATES

"Therefore, a man shall leave his father and his mother and hold fast to his wife, and they shall become one flesh."

Genesis 2:24 (ESV)

November 2000

The road is narrow and beautiful. There is ocean and mountainside—shimmering water and majestic peaks—dramatic, calming, stunning, and peaceful all at the same time. The sun is getting ready to set—and the light is spectacular. You pull over at a small hotel and run inside.

"What's wrong?" I ask, hoping everything is ok.

"I just want to make sure we are going the right way. I'm trying to find a specific place." So much mystery. We are on a surprise weekend getaway to the Big Sur Coast. You pull over and drive down a narrow dirt road which eventually leads to a larger parking area.

"Ok, we walk from here," you whisper. There is a dirt path leading through a wooded area. The path leads to an opening beyond the trees to reveal a stunning beach. The sun is dazzling on the water—lighting up waves of orange, red, and magenta. We sit and stare at the view in silence for a few moments and then decide to go up to touch the water. Ever since I was a little girl, my mom would say, "make sure you respect the ocean" and, somehow, the image of the ocean as a spiritual person would form in my mind. I saw the ocean as a living entity, and for some reason, I had to greet the ocean with respect each time I came to visit. My ritual included walking up to the water, giving thanks, and putting my hands in the water. Once, I said hello and properly greeted the ocean, I felt like I could go on with whatever I was going to do. You knew my ritual by now, and you waited patiently in the sand as I walked up to the water and said hello. A surprise wave came in and my hello was cut short, as I ran back up to you to avoid getting my shoes wet. The November air is crisp and cool.

"Come on, lets walk," I say, and we started walking further out along the beach. There were very few people on that side of the beach, and after walking for a few minutes, you reach over and grab my hand. Something is different. You are quieter than usual, and I look over and try to read the expression on your face. I walk faster, and you pull me closer to you.

"Stop," you say. "I want you to know that I love you." I can feel your heart racing as you pull me closer to you.

"I have never met anyone like you. From the moment we met, I knew we were soulmates, and I have known that you and I would always be together." You let go of my hand, for just a moment, and reach into your jacket pocket and pull out a small black box. You are on one knee now. "Will you do me the honor of becoming my wife and spending the rest of your life with me?"

"Yes," I whisper. I'm in a dream of golden sunsets, soulmates, love, beauty. The view is breathtaking. "Yes, yes, yes…" You slip the ring on my finger and our lips meet. I can hear my own heart thundering in my ears. All the mystery of the surprise weekend—the planning was all for this amazing question. It was a question that had already been answered and settled years prior. We both knew the answer, but we were ready for the world to know. We continue walking and watch the golden ball of fire disappear over the horizon. When we finally make our way to the car, the darkness of the night settles over us. Above the trees, I can see the image of a full moon peek beyond the clouds over us. The sun and the moon. You and I, ready to take on the world.

Tuesday, December 18, 2001

Sweetie,

I just wanted to shoot you a quick email as I had promised. First of all, I want to let you know that I love you with all my heart and soul. RELAX, RELAX, RELAX . . . . . . Remember our love is the only thing that matters, everything else is just trivial. All these little curve balls that are being thrown our way can be dealt with, and we will learn to move on. Once again, the only thing that matters is that we love each other and are going to spend the rest of our lives together. Just imagine that . . . TOGETHER FOR FOREVER. Remember how cheesy that sounded when we were kids, but in a way, it held some truth. Now as adults, through marriage, we are committing to each other for the rest of our lives. AND THAT EXCITES ME!!!!!!!!!!!! I am so looking forward to officially starting our lives together. I was listening to Etta James this morning and that song actually brought a tear to my insensitive ass . . . . The song means so much to me because through marrying you, I feel as if I have reached a milestone in my life. It is finally at last… At last, I have found the love of my life. At last, I have reached a major plateau in my life. Now it is all downhill from here. I have found my soulmate, MY WIFE, MY LOVE, MY EVERYTHING AND BOY AM I EXCITED!!!!!!!!!!!! I am now ready to face the world knowing that I have the most beautiful, intelligent, and loving woman by my side……. I want you to know that I will take the most absolute care of you and will love and cherish you for as long as I shall live, through thick and thin. Sorry about this long email, but I just had to get this out. I have been short of breath lately and I have been wondering why. I have realized it is because I am so excited about becoming one and have so much excitement in me that I do not know how to express it. I am so thrilled!!!!!!! WE WILL HAVE A GREAT LIFE TOGETHER!!!!!!!! I love you and cannot wait to see you and hold you. I hope you get a chance to read this email before I get there. I will see you very soon.

Your husband to be, THE NONERS...........

January 24, 2013

Dear Gabby,

I feel happy and always excited about being married to you. You are my soulmate and best friend. Until I met you, I always felt that people did not understand me. Once I met you, I finally felt, for the first time, that someone finally got me. Being married to you is like always having my best friend by my side.

No matter what happens or what I face throughout the day, I know that I can always call my best friend. Someone that will always love me and understand me—not judge me—and is always looking out for my best interests. Being married to you is like finding my better half and adding that to my personality. You are my soulmate, and I love you with all my heart. Every day is an adventure that I look forward to having with you.

Love,
Nonè

January 24, 2013

Dear Arnoldo,

I love you. You are my soulmate. You are a part of me. I feel so grateful to God to have you in my life. My feelings are like the peace of watching the golden splendor of a sunset, the anticipation of the warmth of the sunrays in the sunrise, and the joy of hearing all of our children's laughter. Peace, warmth, joy, anticipation, hope, faith—love—I love being married to you. I love being a part of you. You make me feel better about me because you love me. God bless you always, Arnoldo! May our marriage continue to grow in love. Imagine us—years from now—Noah and Matthew visiting with their children, bouncing around our house. Imagine the joy. Imagine you and I together in France—driving through the countryside—reading and eating. This is living. This is loving. I love the here, the now, the past, and the future.

Love,
Gabby

May 24, 2013

Dear Arnoldo,

Jesus would want me to pray for your health. You give and give and give so much that you neglect yourself. You give to your job, to your family, to me, and you never ask for anything in return. You are a blessing to us, and I feel that Jesus would want me to pray for you to take care of yourself—physically, emotionally, spiritually. You must not neglect yourself—you are an amazing miraculous person, father, partner, but you must take care of you. In taking care of you—you care for us. I believe Christ needs you to continue your example on earth. Your boys need your loving, giving example. Why else would God have given you boys? Your brothers and father need your example—why else would God have given you the family you have and made you so different? BUT you must take care of yourself and take care of the physical body granted to you. You must also take care of your spiritual needs—feed the soul. Think of you and what YOU need. It is ok to do this because, in the long run, you are taking are of the souls that need your example. We need you. I feel happy to be sharing this with you and relieved. I feel like I have gotten a weight off my shoulders. Light—like when you walk into a pool of water and you feel weightless. I also feel relieved because I know God will allow you to hear his message.

Love,

Gabby

May 24, 2013

Dear Gabby,

I believe Jesus would want me to pray to continue to strengthen your FAITH. Since the day I met you, you have always had very strong faith. You have helped me with seeing the good in others and to not be so judgmental. I feel with what has happened to you with your parents, it is crucial that you remain strong with your faith. I feel that this is what makes you such a beautiful person. You always find the beauty in others.

Every time I think of what happened or listen to you speak about it, I get emotional. I feel a big lump in my throat. I feel angry and helpless that I cannot take that pain away. I wonder how such bad things can happen to such a beautiful person.

I then realize that this is all in God's plan. My purpose is to ensure you stay strong in your FAITH. I must ensure you continue down the path of GOD. Together we can face anything. We keep each other strong.

Love,

Nonè

ANOTHER STEP OF FAITH

"For we live by faith, not by sight."

2 Corinthians 5:7 (NIV)

The ambulance ride from Sacramento to Palo Alto was long and bumpy. It was late in the evening and luckily the rush-hour traffic was long gone. I sat in the ambulance holding Arnoldo's hand. A nurse sat in the back with me. She worked on paperwork in silence. He was deep in drug-induced sleep. The medications he was on were strong and meant to control the *storming* while he was transferred. It was my first time in the back of an ambulance, and I realized, with a sickening feeling, that this was not the first time for Arnoldo. He had been alone while he was being taken to the hospital—while he was dying—while he was fighting for that choice to stay or to go. There had been no one there to hold his hand. He stayed. He had made that choice . . . alone.

I was surprised at how bumpy it was in the back of the emergency vehicle. At one point, the ambulance hit a large pothole and the entire gurney shook. Part of Arnoldo's ventilator came undone, and the surprised nurse scrambled to reconnect it. I held his hand tightly.

"I'm here. I'm here. You are safe," I said softly. I felt my heart beating wildly in my chest. His sister followed behind us, and I could make out the headlights of her car through the hazy back window of the ambulance. I felt the ambulance slow down as it entered the front of the hospital. No one was there to greet us. I walked with the two critical care transport nurses to the main entrance—Arnoldo, still peaceful on the gurney. It was late. My eyes burned with the dryness of the hot air in the ambulance and from the sleepless nights of the past few weeks. Once inside, he was quickly transported to the Neuro-Intensive Care Unit on the second floor. I walked quickly, not wanting to let go of his hand, as we wound through several hallways on our way to the unit. We were greeted by several cheery nurses that quickly introduced themselves and started the admissions paperwork, while another group worked to get Arnoldo safely transferred from his gurney to a bed. I had never been inside this hospital's ICU, but it could not be further from what I imagined. The walls looked dated and worn. The hallways were lit by fluorescent lights and what looked like the ventilation system in the ceiling appeared to have not been updated in decades. The small room held four beds only separated by thin curtains. There was only a small amount of space beside each bed for the nursing staff to come in and attend to their patient. Black and white images of World War II injured soldiers laying in a room full of other patients drifted through my mind. I tried not to look as a nurse attended to a woman in the bed across from Arnoldo. She moaned with pain as her headdress was changed. Once the housekeeping of going through Arnoldo's medication list was completed and all the admissions paperwork was finished, two young doctors walked in. They introduced themselves and began evaluating his chart. They both gasped when they looked at his medication. "He's very comfy," one of them commented. "His sedation is very high. We will need to work to bring that down to a much lower level, to see if he can respond to commands and eventually come out of this." I nodded.

"The other doctors think he was storming. Part of the reason they have him on such high meds is to keep those symptoms controlled." I offered. The doctors nodded and assured me that he would be in the best of hands. His sister and I took turns at his bedside and did not leave the entire night. We had begun a new part of this journey, and the road ahead was dark and perilous. I prayed for light.

Let the morning bring me word of your unfailing love,
for I have put my trust in you.

Psalm 143:8 (NIV)

April 30, 2017

Dear God,

I am crying out to you. I am hurting deeply. I am scared. I have no knowledge of what to do. I've never found myself needing you more. Where are you? By day, I am in the hospital room challenging the doctors, sending them articles, researching more and more information, and keeping them on their toes, regarding what can be done for Arnoldo. I'm learning to speak their language. I'm diving into the medical world. Like it or not, I am battling with the physical reality of dying and illness. I battle and battle and feel as though I cannot win. I am lost. Every night, I drive to my barracks room. It is a room offered to me by a good friend who has access to these old military rooms. The cost is low, and they are very close to the hospital. It is past midnight—dark and so lonely. The rooms are barren but complete—just a small light, a twin bed and a bathroom. There is no television in the room, and it allows for nothing but silence and reflection.

A few days ago, a beautiful friend offered to give me a massage free of charge. She is a masseuse and wanted to give me the gift of relaxation. I agreed and fell into a deep state of relaxation. I felt myself holding back tears as I drifted in and out of sleep. Presently, I heard a voice speaking directly to me. There was no doubt it was for me because the voice said, "Gabby, Gabby, it will be ok. He will be ok." I felt myself awaken and thought that maybe someone had entered the room . . . but there was the voice again. This time, I heard it clearly, and I was awake. "Gabby, he will be ok." It was a voice that was in my head, but it was super clear. It is hard to put into words, since the words came into my thoughts and not through my ears. "Who are you?" I felt myself asking the voice. I didn't speak out loud. The question just formed in my head. "I am Mother Mary, and I am here to tell you that your husband, Arnoldo, will be ok—he will be healed." I felt the weight of despair and fear lift from my shoulders. When the massage was complete, I shared what I had heard with my friend. God, was that Mary? Was that Mary bringing me comfort? Was that my own subconscious trying to find a survival mechanism and search for a scrap of hope? Please, Father God, tell me. I believe it was. I believe she came to give me the comfort that only a mother can.

Thank you for sending her. I needed that message and hold on to it dearly. God, after her message, I began hearing your voice more clearly and more often. In my drives to and from the hospital, I kept hearing your voice, and your message is always the same . . . it is always one of comfort. It is always one of a promise of healing for Arnoldo. I'm sorry for my outburst the other day. I'm sorry for yelling at you. I'm sorry for not showing gratitude day by day. Forgive me. I keep hearing your voice tell me that Arnoldo will be ok, and I arrive at the hospital and see my strong husband sweating, writhing, moaning, coughing. The "storming" is in full force. His heart rate is extreme, his blood pressure is dangerously high, he is covered in sweat morning and night, and the doctors try and try to find a way to control his "storming" symptoms to no avail. I heard you one night tell me to begin to massage his feet. I did, and he began to calm down. Thank you, Lord, for helping me—for holding my hand through this. I am struggling with my faith; and even though I hear your voice clearly giving me comfort, I am always in doubt. Help me to believe without seeing. Increase my faith and take my fear. I've never felt so alone. Arnoldo is my partner. He is my soulmate, and I feel lost without him. Help me, God, to rely on you and to begin to see that the physical world does not matter because through you anything can be done. Lord, increase my faith. I accept your promise of healing for Arnoldo, and I hear your words. Thank you.

Love,
Your Daughter,
Gabby

May 1, 2017

We had a family meeting with the doctors. They sat us down in a small room—his mother and father, his brothers and sisters. They brought in a translator for his parents, and the neurologists at Stanford put on a power point for our benefit. It was the MRI image of Arnoldo's brain. They went over each part of his brain and told us where the damage was.

"He will most likely be blind."

"He will never come out of his vegetative state."

"He will never be able to walk."

"He will not respond or know you."

As they talked, we listened. I saw his dad wiping tears, his mom sitting with a stoic look on her face, and his siblings sitting in silence. In my head, I could hear my own voice screaming, "Yes, but what about God?" They were discounting God. They stated that the odds of Arnoldo ever being healed were low, but God is not of this world. God is the ultimate healer and through him anything is possible. I felt his presence in that meeting, and I knew that what I was hearing was *not true*. They had forgotten God. Arnoldo would wake up. He would know us. He would walk again and eat again and be my partner in this life. God had promised it, and I was holding on to that promise.

F.R.O.G.
(FULLY RELY ON GOD)

"Trust in the Lord with all your heart, and do not lean on your own understanding."

Proverbs 3:5 (ESV)

Eve, my dear friend that was with us the day of Arnoldo's sudden cardiac arrest, was often the friend I called on the lonely drives back to my barren room on the old military base near the hospital. She often stayed on the phone with me until I was safely inside my room with the doors locked. The drive from the hospital to the room wasn't far, but once on the base, it was dark, and she wanted to ensure my safety. I was grateful for the company, and because I wasn't used to being alone, I welcomed the conversation. Many of our conversations turned to God and how God was using this situation for his glory. She had full faith that Arnoldo would make a full recovery, and she assured me that those words that I heard on a daily basis from God, were not in vain. I often recounted to her my struggles with faith and with being one hundred percent dependent on God. I had always been very independent and always felt that if I put my mind to something, I could accomplish it. This situation had struck our family a devastating blow, and I found myself completely helpless for the first time in my life. It was as if I was suddenly thrust into a dark ocean and the only hand for me to grasp was

God's. So, I did. It wasn't easy at first, but as I began to trust less in myself and more in him, I felt a peace that I had never felt before. I began to feel calm, and at times, I would recount to him my struggles and concerns and felt that he would always reply to me.

"You are FROG-in' it!" Eve happily declared one night on my drive.

"What do you mean?" I asked.

"Fully relying on God, "FROG-ing" is what we used to call it. It is the way we all should live every day." I reflected on those words and on the power of those words. To *fully* rely on God would mean never being afraid, never worrying, never living in a state of guilt or shame or anger. Fully relying on God is simply that—giving everything to him, everything for him, and letting go of the human restraints that often blind us and bind us to the point of defeat. I had never in my life lived this way and here I was, completely forced to. I contemplated that this is the way EVERYONE should live—not just when faced with trials and tribulations, but with everyday life. Our life should be his and every action should be for him. If God is love and everything is done in love, for love and given to love—why would we in any way ever feel fear or sadness or anger? This earth would be filled with compassion and love. It was liberating to discover this, and I found myself wanting to share this message. I felt God's peace when I gave him my sorrow. Oh, if only I can remember this every second of every day. What peace there would be.

One morning, as I prayed before heading to the hospital, I felt as though God asked me to open the Bible. I did, and my eyes landed on Psalm 40. I read through the scripture, and as I read, I had a vision of Arnoldo and I standing in front of a great congregation, speaking about God and faith. The vision was so real. I read through the Psalm again and I saw the following:

"I have told the glad news of deliverance in the great congregation; behold, I have not restrained my lips, as you know, O Lord. I have not hidden your

deliverance within my heart, I have spoken of your faithfulness and your salvation; I have not concealed your steadfast love and your faithfulness from the great congregation." (Psalm 40:9 ESV)

I felt such joy in my heart to know that God had such an amazing plan for us. I felt at peace knowing this and seeing my Arnoldo fully recovered and standing before the world. It made what I saw and heard on a daily basis at Stanford much easier to tolerate.

Every day, I would massage Arnoldo's hands and feet, and I often would ask him if he could hear me, to squeeze my hand or lift his arms or legs. There were times when he would not move; but often, I would see his leg moving—ever so slightly. We quickly came to realize several things. He had much more control over his legs than his arms or hands. Secondly, he was much more responsive to my voice than to anyone else's. Every day, the neuro-intensivist team would come into his room early in the morning. The team included the attending physician and a group of residents. Each day a new resident was asked to present Arnoldo to the team: his injuries, ailments, medications, progress, etc. At first, it was torture to hear over and over and over the same story. After a few weeks, it became routine, and I would not cringe at hearing: *"This is Arnoldo Avila, 42-year-old male. He suffered a sudden cardiac arrest while driving with his wife and three children and a subsequent anoxic brain injury......"* Every day, the doctors would shine a light in his eyes, pinch his feet, and yell in his ears.

"Mr. Avila, can you hear me? Mr. Avila, if you can hear me, can you please give me a thumbs up?" Their voice always thundered through the unit, and I always thought to myself, he's in a coma, he isn't deaf. Each time, Arnoldo was perfectly still, and their assembly would exit. Every day, I would tell the doctors that he had moved his leg at the sound of my voice, and every day they gave me a look of pity and sadness. I didn't care, I stood perfectly still, tall, and serious. "It has happened enough times for me to know that it is not a reflex, and it is not a coincidence. You come in for five minutes and leave. I am here every day, and I know what I am seeing. Still, the look from them was of pity and condescension. It wasn't until a friend suggested that I record what I was seeing, that things changed.

"Gabby record it. Keep asking him to move his leg and see if you can catch it on video. They cannot deny a video." Great advice. I started to record each time I would ask him to move his left leg or right leg. There was often no movement, but one morning—he moved—and he moved every time I asked. Sometimes the movements were slight and other times his leg would clearly raise up over his bed. I had explained to him that the doctors did not believe that he could hear me and that they were starting to give up. I told him I was recording, and he responded every single time. The next morning, when the doctors came in, I was ready. They went through the regular routine of introducing "Mr. Avila" and presenting his case. When they were done yelling in his ear and asking him to give them a thumbs up, I pulled aside the attending doctor and shared with her what I had seen. The look of pity formed around her eyes.

"Wait, I have a video taken yesterday for you." The team gathered around my cell phone and watched as Arnoldo raised his left leg over and over.

"Do you think you can ask him to do that right now?" she asked. I walked over to his bedside and gently rubbed his arm.

"Arnoldo, if you can hear me, please raise your left leg. The team of neurologists are here, and they want to know that you can hear me." His leg twitched and came up—ever so slightly. There was a gasp among them.

"This is good," the attending doctor reported. "It doesn't mean much until he completely wakes up, but this is very good." I stood straight and tall. We had their attention now. They saw hope too and that was important. They wouldn't give up now. The adrenaline rushed through my veins. I could fight too.

"Yes, it is very good," I answered.

Many months later, a friend of mine confided that she knew someone that worked at the hospital and had reached out to him to find out about Arnoldo. Her contact had written back and said that Arnoldo was on the *Organ Donor* list. In fact, he was on the docket to have someone speak to his family about donating. They did not expect him to live, but God had a different plan.

Dear Matthew,

When you came into the world, a few things happened. Our hearts grew bigger because your dada and I loved more than we ever thought possible. Your sweet little face and body would snuggle next to me every night, and dada slept with Noah to keep him company and make sure he got a full night's sleep. Our little family of three grew to four, and it was beautiful. In an instant, Noah became a big brother and your dad and mom were the proud parents of two beautiful boys! Dad worked extra hard at work to give you and Noah the things you needed, and mom worked from home too and eventually decided to stay home completely to be with you. We needed a bigger house and started looking, and soon, we moved to our beautiful community of Brentwood. You were my little buddy, and you went with me every day to pick up Noah from school. I love you with all my heart and soul. Your sweet smile and your silliness are all a momma needs to make her feel better. Dad also loved that you used to wait up for him to come home before going to sleep. Dad was going to school during this time and would come home late a few nights per week. You were just a little baby, but you needed that Dada hug and kiss and would love to get tucked into your crib by him. It made his heart swell with pride and joy to know that his little boy was waiting up for him. Thank you for being you. Thank you for bringing so much joy, laughter, and love to our lives. Keep loving. Keep sharing your joy with others. It is infectious, and it will change the world. Dad loves his happy little Tigger so much! Don't EVER FORGET THAT!

Love,

Mom

June 2010

I will never forget when the anxiety started. The postpartum depression really started several months after Noah was born. He was born January 3, 2007 and by January 8th I was back in school. It was my last year of law school, and I couldn't afford to take any time off. My mother came to help, and with her help with the baby, I completed my last semester and graduated. A few weeks after graduation, I was back at work. My mom left for home, and I navigated the waters of being home alone with my new baby. Noah and I would commute every day from South San Jose to Mountain View. I would drop him off early in the morning at the onsite day care and pick him up in the evening. By the time we got home, there was barely enough time for dinner and bedtime. Arnoldo always came home after he fell asleep. Looking back, I realize that I never really had the necessary mother-baby bonding time with him. I never relaxed—I had finals two weeks before he was born, and I was back in school right after. At the time, it was worth it. I had started a law career, and I kept telling myself that it was for our family's betterment. Then the depression hit. It started slowly—small pangs of fear when I would leave the house with the baby. Then, it was sudden feelings of sadness at work—this eventually turned to anxiety and the inability to think clearly. Arnoldo was deep into his business career and offered little help. I remember talking to him about how I was feeling, about all my fears, and he would look at me like I was an alien. "You will be fine," he said. "Everything will be fine." That was his answer to everything. It wasn't enough for me. I couldn't shake the feeling that something was wrong—that something was off. As time went on, I couldn't work full-time anymore, and I was granted permission to work from home part time. I went about hiring a nanny to take care of Noah while I worked. For a while, this system worked. I was home, Noah was home, and things seemed to be manageable. When Matthew was born, I took some much-needed time off. This time though, the anxiety hit where I least expected it.

"Please call in," I pleaded.

"Gabby, I can't. I Need to work." Arnoldo's eyes looked tired, and his voice had an edge of irritation.

"I know, but I just need you to stay here. Don't leave. Please don't leave," I answered.

It was three o'clock in the morning. We had been up all night arguing. I wanted Arnoldo to stay home. He argued that I was being unreasonable. He needed to work. He was right. There was no *reason* for the way I was feeling. I just couldn't shake the feeling that something terrible would happen to Arnoldo. I envisioned a terrible car accident, a drive-by shooting, an illness. Matthew was only a few months old when I started having anxiety about Arnoldo. Whenever Arnoldo would leave for work, I panicked. This time, he listened and asked me to get some help. I did and was able to work through my anxiety with counseling. For many years, the fear of something happening to him was gone.

It resurfaced in the Spring of 2016. One year prior, almost to the day, to his sudden cardiac arrest. During that time, I had a deep fear of losing him. It tormented me, and I couldn't shake the feeling. It wasn't until I prayed and had a vision of our little family in our home—Matthew and Noah were walking through the door, and they were older, like high school or even college age, Nico was a preteen, and Arnoldo and I were sitting at the table as they walked in, and Arnoldo stood up in joy to greet them—that I felt as though I could get a glimpse into the future. I felt calmer and the fear of losing him left me.

One year later, as I sat in the hospital just a few days following his cardiac arrest, praying for his recovery, I remembered the vision. I saw him at the table, sitting in our kitchen, as our boys entered our home. We were all together—under one roof. This is the vision I held onto—this is God's promise. Arnoldo will wake up. He will recover. He will come home. To God be the glory when this happens.

THE KISSES WE NEVER SAW COMING

"The LORD will fight for you, and you have only to be silent."

Exodus 14:14 (ESV)

May 9, 2017

Drops of dried blood surrounded very swollen tissue that held the tube in Arnoldo's neck. It had been a few days since Arnoldo had a tracheotomy and gastrostomy. The tracheotomy involved an incision in his throat where a tube that was connected to a machine was inserted to continue to help him breathe. The gastrostomy was the placement of a tube inside his stomach. This was to ensure that he received nutrition and fluids while he was in a coma. The day after his surgery, I inspected his neck to see if his birthmark was still in place, and I felt relieved to see that it was still there. The birthmark was the shape of a star, and it sat directly to the right of his Adam's apple. I know it was silly to worry about his birthmark remaining in place—yet, somehow holding on to the smaller things, the familiar, was the only way I could feel that sense of comfort. So much had changed in such a short time. I had kissed his birthmark hundreds of times over the past years. Each of our boys had snuggled against it as they wrapped their arms around his neck, and they had all come to know it as part of him. By now, he had been moved several times throughout the ICU and was now in a private room. The hospital had decided that due to the level of coughing and suctioning, he would need to be closely monitored and kept him in ICU.

In ICU, the nursing staff was inside his room most of the time. His room was between two other private rooms and was divided by glass doors and privacy curtains. His neighbor on one side was a young man that was also in a coma. His room was covered with photographs of his life prior to whatever trauma had ensued. Smiling photos of him on his jet skis, surfing, him on his motorcycle and laughing with friends were plastered on one side of the glass wall. His mother and wife were there most days, talking to him and urging him to wake up. The room on the other side of Arnoldo's was always covered by the privacy curtain. The nurse in Arnoldo's room this afternoon was a young, dark-haired woman who quietly did her computer work at her station. His mother and father had left for the day, and I stayed by his bedside alone. I played music, massaged his body and talked to him. His thumb on his left hand had become very stiff and contracted, and I worked slowly, massaging gently. Presently, I heard my phone ringing and I could see that it was coming from our home phone. It was our boys, calling in to say goodnight. For the past several weeks, they would call just before bed to say goodnight. In the past, Arnoldo was always in charge of the bedtime routine in our house and they missed his bedtime stories, giggles, and prayers. I tried my best over the phone to chat with them about their day and to hear about their school adventures. Noah was planning for his first overnight trip with his class. I could hear the sadness in his voice. "You ready to say goodnight to dad?" I asked. Matthew and Nico had already said their goodbyes.

"Yeah," Noah's voice sounded wistful. I put the phone on speaker and placed it near Arnoldo's ear.

"Hi Dad. It's me Noah. How are you doing? I can't wait for you to wake up. I can't wait for you to come home. School is going ok. Everyone is all excited for Sutter's Fort. I hope you can get better in time for that." My heart sank. Sutter's Fort was just a few weeks away, and I knew

Arnoldo would not be better by then. "Well, I wanted to tell you that every time I hear an ambulance siren or see one go by, I say a prayer. I say a prayer for the people inside the ambulance, but I also say a prayer for their family. It's just that I now know how they feel. Anyway, Dad, I'm going to say goodnight now and give you your blessing. You always used to kiss me and say goodnight and, well, since you can't do it, I'm going to kiss you and say goodnight. I miss you kissing me goodnight. I miss your bedtime stories and jokes." His voice cracked; he was sobbing now. "I can't wait until you come home, Dad, and can kiss me goodnight. Bye." Tears were running down my face, as I picked up the phone and said goodnight to my Noah.

"It will be ok, Noah," I said quietly.

"I'm sorry, Mom. I always try to be cheerful and tell Dad good things. But today, I just feel so sad, and I really miss him."

"I know that baby. I know, and it is ok to feel that way." I wiped my tears and saw that the nurse was wiping tears from her face. I said goodbye to Noah and placed my phone back in my purse.

"I'm so sorry," she said. "Is that your oldest son?"

"Yes."

"He's so strong. Arnoldo has so much to fight for..."

"Yes, he does," I whispered. I sat in my chair quietly, reflecting on the moment. A few weeks back, we had all gone for a walk together—Arnoldo and I, the boys, and our dog, *Duke*. One of our favorite pastimes was walking. The boys loved riding their scooters up ahead and we would follow behind with the baby in the stroller, the dog on a leash. I remembered a time, before we had kids, when I had seen a dad jogging with a baby in a red jogger stroller. The baby was barefoot and sat gleefully in pure bliss while the wind hit his little chubby feet—legs extended, toes wiggling. The dad held onto a red leash—with a golden Labrador Retriever by his side. I remember thinking how much I wanted that for Arnoldo—for us. How much I wanted us to be parents. When it happened, and we had our own jogger stroller and baby, it was almost surreal. I felt whole, content, happy, and at the same time, fiercely anxious and protective. To see Arnoldo missing out on this life—our life, together with our boys—was too much. He had so much to live for. The sound of moaning and screaming in the next room brought me out of my thoughts. The nurse looked up and quickly ran out of the room. I could hear wailing and moaning, and I saw people running in and out of the room next door. The sound of Arnoldo's blood pressure cuff made a whirring noise, and I looked over at him. His face was still—peacefully still in the deep sleep of a coma. It had been several days since he had "stormed," and I felt at peace knowing his brain was calming. The doors opened, and the nurse came back in to check on him.

"Is everything ok?" I asked. She looked flushed and anxiously fidgeted with her hands.

"The patient next door just passed. I'm going to need to fill out some paperwork and speak to the family. Please press the button if you need anything." I nodded, my heart filling with dread at the thought that a life was here and was gone so fast.

What is happening God? Why am I here in this place? Just a few weeks ago, the most complicated thing in my life was choosing the meal of the day and whether it was time for a new couch in our living room. Now, I am in my husband's hospital room listening to the wailing of a family that has just lost their loved one. I have never in my life felt so alone, so vulnerable, and in such despair. God, what is happening?

My heart filled with sadness, anger, despair. As I got up, ready to leave for the night and return to my simple military barracks room, I made a decision. The boys had not seen their father since the week of Arnoldo's cardiac arrest. It was clear that they needed to see him, and with life hanging so delicately by a thread, I dreaded the thought of them not seeing him again. I would take them out of school the next day and bring them to him. I kissed Arnoldo's cheek and whispered in his ear.

"Your boys will be here tomorrow, Arnoldo. Please wake up. They love you and need you so much. I love you. Good night."

The next day, I met my brother in the lobby of the ICU. It was May 10, 2017. *Mexican Mother's Day*. In Mexico, Mother's Day is always celebrated on May 10th, regardless of the day of the week. The boys hugged me and gave me a small gift.

"Happy Mexican Mother's Day, Mommy!" I hugged them tight. It had been several days since I had seen them, and it felt so good to bring them close and feel their warm bodies pressed against mine.

"Hi, babies, how are you?"

"Good, we want to see Dada. Is he awake yet?"

"No, not yet, but keep praying. It will happen." Noah nodded. He looked much better than I had imagined.

"Can we go?" he asked.

"Sure, but if anyone asks, you are twelve years old." The ICU had a strict policy that no children under twelve were allowed in the unit. I had to figure out how to sneak them past the desk. "Wait here with your Uncle and let me go see how Dad's doing."

I walked back into the ICU room and spoke to Arnoldo's nurse for the dayshift. I was ready for a fight with the hospital administration if I needed to take it that far. Our boys would see their father.

"His boys are here to see him. They may not be able to get another chance to see their father alive. I hope you will not object." To my surprise, she agreed, with the condition that they come in one at a time and not cause too much noise or disturbance on the floor. I walked Noah in first, avoiding the main Nurses' Station. "You ready, buddy?" He nodded.

"I'm just worried about the tube in his neck. Is it bloody?" His eyes were filled with concern.

"No, it's ok. Remember, he may look different, but all those tubes are there to help him breath. Just talk to him, Noah. He can hear you. He may not be able to respond, but he can hear you." Noah nodded. Noah walked in and took his father's hand in his. He kissed his cheek and stroked the hairs on his arms. He talked to him about school, about Halloween, about video games and friends and teachers and all the things that a ten-year-old boy would think to say to his father that was in a coma fighting for his life. I let him talk, and when he was finished, I walked him out to get Matthew.

"Hi, Dada," our six-year-old son said hesitantly, as he looked at all the tubes and machines. I explained what each one did and why it was important to have them. This seemed to alleviate any apprehension he might have had. "When are you going to wake up, Dada? I miss you." His dark curly hair snuggled against his father's left arm. "I can't wait to have you come home." He looked up at me, his eyes bright with tears. "Can we go eat now? I'm hungry."

"Yes, of course, baby. Let's go." I led him back to his older brother in the waiting room. We agreed to have lunch and then to go look at the toy train in the Children's Hospital. I left with them and felt an air of relief. They had seen their father. It may be the last time, or it may not. The future was uncertain. Nevertheless, I relished the moment and scooped up each one in my arms and kissed them tightly. After our meal, and walking around the brightly colored Children's Hospital, I walked them back to the waiting area to say goodbye. They had school the next day, and I didn't want them to be up too late. My brother was packing up their school things, and I ushered them in to say goodbye to their father for the night. Matthew kissed him and rubbed his arm and ran out to get his brother. Noah rubbed his father's arm gently and kissed his hand.

"Good night, Dada," he whispered. "How I wish you could kiss me good night like you used to, but I understand. I know you will one day. I love you, and I have to go now, but I will come back soon." His eyes filled with tears and my own eyes stung. I felt my pain turn to anger, and I walked over to Arnoldo and whispered in his ear.

"Don't you hear your son? Don't you hear your son, asking for a goodnight kiss? Wake up for heaven's sake and give him the kiss he's asking for! He's hurting so much. We all are . . . " I was sobbing now.

"Mom, Mom . . . look!" Noah's voice was shrill. I looked up to see that Arnoldo had lifted his head from his pillow and had brought his lips into a pucker, wanting to give the kiss that Noah so desperately needed. His arms lifted halfway off the bed.

"Oh! Oh, my God! Noah, he's trying to give you a goodnight kiss!" I cried. Sure enough, he turned his head toward Noah's voice, and Noah leaned in to receive his father's kiss. As soon as his lips touched his son's face, he fell back onto the bed. I was sobbing. We had both witnessed a miracle. Arnoldo could hear us, and he was fighting; fighting to make his way back to the land of the living to be with his children and with me. Noah and I ran out to the waiting room, too excited to even speak.

"Que pasa?" His mother looked anxious as she saw my face.

"He's waking up—it's actually happening . . . " Everyone rushed into the room. Arnoldo was still once again. Eyes closed, machines whirring— just as it had been. His mother looked confused as she stood in the doorway.

"Arnoldo, today is Mexican Mother's Day. Your mother is here and would love a kiss for Mother's Day. If you can hear me, please give her a kiss to let her know you love her." I prayed for movement. He lifted his head off the pillow, his lips pursed in a kiss, his arms extended. She gasped, and I saw his father wiping away tears. "It's happening . . . it's really happening," I whispered. Matthew squealed in delight! "Dada's waking up!" Thus, the beginning of Arnoldo's rebirth into the world—brought back by the desire to kiss his first-born son goodnight and to hug and kiss his mother and sons.

IN LESS THAN ONE YEAR

"We are afflicted in every way, but not crushed; perplexed, but not driven to despair; persecuted, but not forsaken; struck down, but not destroyed"

2 Corinthians 4:8-9 (ESV)

October 2010

I remember the phone call well. My mom and I spoke on the phone every day. Our second son, Matthew, had just been born and we were in the process of closing on a new home in a new town. She was excited for us and had lots of questions about our new house, moving date, and new town.

"What about Ozma? You think she will be ok? Where will you put her?" Princess Ozma was our beautiful black, mini-panther, Burmese-mix cat. She was 10 years old.

"Yeah, mom, of course she will be ok. She always adjusts fine. She's moved plenty of times in the past," I answered. We went on to talk about our many moves and adventures with our Ozma. For a second, mom paused and then she asked me a few questions about our new town. Then she asked again,

"What about Ozma? You think she will be ok? Where will you put her?"

"Mom, you already asked me that." We had just finished talking about her.

"I did? I don't think so." Mom sounded confused. "Well, ok. Yeah, I think I just forgot." My heart sank. What was going on? She had never done this before. Just the previous day, we had spent twenty minutes on the phone exchanging recipes. Well, it was more like she was giving me step by step instructions on how to make her delicious *fideo*, which is a Mexican comfort food. I was just learning to cook, and she was always a quick phone call away for advice. Once we got off the phone, I called my dad at work to ask if he had noticed anything strange.

"I knew you would be the one to notice first," he answered. His voice sounded defeated and despondent.

"When did you notice? What's going on? Why didn't you tell me right away?" I went into panic mode.

"Gabby, I just wasn't sure what was happening. She's been confused over the past couple of weeks. She's also very anxious. She can't sleep. Her shoulders keep twitching and her legs cramp. We thought it was a muscular issue, but now I'm not sure."

"Dad, we need to take her to the emergency department. It might be a stroke."

"I never thought it might be that. In my mind, I think it's Alzheimer's."

"Dad, it doesn't happen this way. It never does. Alzheimer's is gradual. Mom's symptoms are sudden." I was going over dates in my mind and realized she had been at our house just a few weeks prior. Nothing seemed wrong at the time, other than some muscle cramps in her legs.

This was the beginning of my mother's illness. Within two weeks, most of her recent memories disappeared. Within a month's time, she began hallucinating and eventually began losing her ability to talk and walk. Local doctors were stumped. She had not suffered a stroke and Alzheimer's was ruled out. Her case was transferred to another hospital, and they immediately began more extensive testing. A small tumor was discovered in her lung. It was cancer. In addition, tests had come back that she had Lymbic Encephalitis. Essentially, her own antibodies were attacking healthy brain cells. Mom was scheduled for surgery to remove the tumor in her lung. She was scheduled for various treatments and infusions. She could no longer take care of herself, so she stayed in our new home while she healed. She didn't know who Arnoldo was, or who our children were. She always knew me, and for that I was grateful. Arnoldo shouldered my pain, my anguish and confusion. I hated not knowing and not understanding what was happening. My dad's heart was broken. He was confused and lost without my mother. On October 7, 2011—one year after that first phone call, my father died of a massive heart attack on his way to work. He was alone and it happened on the highway, just minutes from their home. He had managed to pull his car over and put it in neutral. The car was still on when he was found over six hours later. My world was so dark. I felt as though I had already lost my mother—her body was there but her mind was gone. With my father's death, I felt as though I was an orphan. In less than one year, both of them were gone.

Three days after my father's death, my mother began talking. We were mystified because prior to this her attempts to speak were confused and incoherent. She told us that my father had come to her in a dream and that he had reassured her that he would be ok and that all of us in their home would be blessed. Once the dream was shared, my mother's speech returned to what it was. A heaviness lifted from our home after she shared her dream. Our grief was still deep, but the despair we all felt was gone.

Whenever I thought of their small ranch house in the countryside, my heart felt pangs of sorrow-filled pain. Their house sits on three acres amidst orchards of peaches, walnuts, and prunes. There are no streetlights, and the only illumination is from the night sky. One of my favorite memories is driving to their home on their dark street and seeing the lights blazing through the windows, my mother bustling about in the kitchen while my father sits reading at the dining room table. Their home now sat empty and cold. There were no smells of baked goods coming from the kitchen, no silky sounds of jazz music from the living room. No booming laughter or sounds of quiet conversation. All is silent in this house. In just a moment's time, the life it once had was extinguished.

I slipped into a deep sadness, and Arnoldo was the rock that I clung to in my sorrow. He encouraged me to get closer to God. My best friend, my flesh—he suffered what I suffered, and I know that he tried all he could to take away my pain. At times, it was too much. God and I began to talk again, and I began to pray and pray. Arnoldo guided me to have alone time, to go on spiritual retreats, to pray more and to seek answers. Years later, I realized that he was grieving too. Arnoldo loved my father like his own. He always said that he was the example of the type of father he strived to be for our children. I didn't know it at the time, as I was deeply self-involved in my own pain. During this time, my parents were empty nesters. My brothers were away at college and because Arnoldo and I lived close, we would visit often. We had many dinners with them and spent many weekends with them. My mother and father were so proud of our accomplishments and let us know often. When our children were born, their love and involvement with them grew even more. I am so grateful now to have had that time with them in that way. At the time, I just felt that our lives would go on forever. Life has a way of reminding us that nothing is forever.

I have often reflected on how fleeting moments can be—both good ones and bad. Until this time of loss and illness, my life had been peaceful and unaffected. I was a child filled with joy, peace, and comfort. Arnoldo brought me a new sense of comfort as a husband and provider—an easy, comfortable life. When the storm came, Arnoldo led me to God. Without God, I would have drowned in my own sorrow. Arnoldo encouraged me to cling to God, he prayed for me each and every day.

When God speaks to us, it is usually with a sense of peaceful authority—a reassurance, a strength that is equal to none. God spoke to me throughout my life, and I didn't recognize that it was him. It wasn't until my mother's illness and my father's death that I began to really hear him and recognize his voice. I have no doubt that he was there all along, but my sorrow and pain led me to quiet moments with him.

I'll never forget seeing a vision of my mother in a gray pantsuit, smiling, laughing and holding a brown suitcase. I had a sense of knowing, in that moment, that she would be healed, and she would one day happily travel back and forth from her house in Mexico to her house in the U.S. When I had this vision, my father had already died, my mother was at her worst—completely incoherent and unable to care for herself. We had hired caregivers to provide her with 24-hour care in my home. The vision was strong, and I knew she would be ok.

Six years later, my mother was by my side caring for our three boys, while I sat by Arnoldo's bedside night after night. To the surprise of all the neurologists, she was healed. God had a higher purpose for her, and despite the impossibility of her illness, she was destined to be here. God's miracles happen every day. Nothing is impossible with God.

THAT'S BECAUSE
THIS IS GOD

"With man this is impossible, but with God all things are possible."

Matthew 19:26 (NIV)

May 2017

There is a spot on the second floor of the hospital that is filled with rays of sunlight in the late afternoon. Dollops of sunlight dot the old leather-lined chairs that line the wall. The windows along this part of the hospital look out to the front courtyard. The front of the hospital is adorned with pools of water and fountains, roses and a tree-lined street. From here, the world looks *normal* and *happy*. People coming and going—laughing, eating lunch, talking. There is a vibrant energy at this hospital that does not exist in other places. An energy of learning, seeking of knowledge, excitement—the heavy rigor of academia, coupled with a youthful energy that can only exist in a teaching hospital. In the afternoons, while Arnoldo's parents say their goodbyes to their son, I sit along this wall and rest. Sometimes, I follow up on insurance phone calls, or catch up on emails. These days, with Arnoldo not working, I am on the phone most of the day trying to figure out how to apply for different benefits. Today, I am sitting with my eyes closed. My head is against the wall, and I can feel the warmth of the sun on my face. It has been several weeks since *the kiss* and Arnoldo has now started to respond to the doctors as well. That morning, they had asked him to turn his head to the left and right and he was able to do both. He was able to lift his left leg and right leg, stick out his tongue and lift his head off the pillow when prompted. I didn't need to see the smile on the attending neurologist's face to know that this was incredible.

"Hello," I heard a familiar voice. I opened my eyes and saw one of the residents on the Neuro-ICU team.

"Hi, Doctor," I responded.

"What he's doing right now, the way he's responding… it NEVER happens this way with his type of injury. It's very unusual. Most patients remain in a vegetative state. This is very good." I smiled and nodded, and in my head, I heard a voice say, *that's because this is God. Tell her.* I wasn't sure what to say, so I didn't say anything. She walked away and I felt ashamed at myself for not obeying. I know it was God. He wanted me to shout from the rooftops. To acknowledge him, to praise him. I had failed. I reminded myself not to allow that to happen again. My relationship with him was much closer now. He spoke to me every day—especially on my drives alone. For a few weeks, I stayed in the military barracks. But then, through a connection of friends, a woman who did not know me, offered up a room in her home in Palo Alto for me to use, as needed. She was in her eighties and had recently lost her husband. I rarely saw her, as I would arrive late at night after staying by Arnoldo's side all day. However, she would often leave a glass of water, flowers, or a kind note by my bedside. It was the relief and love I yearned for—and to God, I am ever so grateful. He reminded me in some way, each day, through the loving acts of people all around us that he was constantly there.

Arnoldo continued to improve. Several weeks later, therapists began to work with him on movement and speech. Despite him having a trach still in place, the therapists were able to place a special device in that allowed him to speak. One of the first words he spoke was *Noah.* It was then followed by *Matthew* and *Nico*. He began saying *hi* and *hey*, and with the help of the therapists, he began to slowly say more and more words. His sisters texted me one morning to say that he was able to sing the *Happy Birthday* song along with them. Each day was a new miracle. I remember observing him one day as he lay in bed. His eyes were open, and he was focusing on his arms. He had just begun to move them again, and he slowly brought them up above his head and then brought his hands together. A new milestone! He reminded me of a newborn infant discovering the world. In so many ways, this was a new birth. Arnoldo had been given a second chance at life. He was reborn into a new experience. There was excitement at watching him. His storming episodes had subsided significantly, and he seemed to become more alert each day.

The hospital began talking with me about moving him to a long-term acute care hospital, and I fought to keep him there. Moving him would not be good. He was so delicate. He needed more time. I have learned many lessons, but there is one lesson that is vital to this entire process, and it is that Personal Advocacy is *essential* for the well-being of patients. This world of medicine, hospitals, and healthcare in general, has become such a financial, industrial machine, that it would seem as though the individual patient is simply a cog in its giant wheel. It was here that I began to understand the complexity of the *Case Manager's* job. A hospital case manager was introduced to me and we spent some time talking about Arnoldo's case. In all, it was about fifteen minutes. She then began to insist that it was time to move him out. Her arguments: He was ready, he didn't need the expertise of the hospital anymore, and that he just needed time to recover.

As I resisted, insurance was brought up over and over—*insurance won't cover his stay here anymore. You will be liable. The hospital needs the bed for other patients.* I didn't feel that I had a choice. I didn't know how to fight what seemed to be inevitable. The case managers all smiled and nodded along and seemed to be concerned with the well-being of

Arnoldo. The reality was that they needed him to move along—to be gone and empty the bed for someone else. Their loyalty belonged to their employer—the hospital. Arnoldo and I were on our own. Brain injuries are complex and take months of recovery. At this point in the conversation, it had been 7 weeks. His move seemed inevitable, and I relented. Arnoldo was moved to a long-term acute care hospital on May 23, 2017.

June 1, 2017

Dear Arnoldo,

I am fighting with every ounce that I have. Every day, I put on my armor. I imagine myself strapping on boots, a shield, a sword, and a breastplate. Every day, I am a warrior, ready to face what is to come. It has been several days since your move to the new hospital. The moment the EMTs wheeled you inside this place, I felt a knot in the pit of my stomach. The entrance to the building is clean and tidy. Metal sofas and chairs fill the space and a worn wooden coffee table greets guests with flowers and pamphlets. Wooden paneling lines the walls, along with various photos of past patients in various stages of their recovery. There is a woman sitting at a modern looking desk in the middle of the lobby. She smiles politely at all who enter. There are no guests sitting in the chairs, and I am overcome with a feeling of sadness and despair. The wheels of the gurney squeak along the stone floor, and as we enter the recovery floor, we are greeted by the smell of urine and feces mixed with a pungent antiseptic. Sounds of moaning and screaming are heard from various rooms and what sounds like sirens can be heard up and down the hallway. Later, I learned that the sirens are the *call alarms* for nursing staff.

Very little staff could be seen along the corridors. The EMTs settled you into your new bed in your new shared room. The room is large and empty. The chipped stone walls are painted a light blue with a dark blue trim. Some of the paint has faded beyond recognition and in other places there are remnants of sticky film—no doubt left by tape or glue—relics of past patients. One wall is lined with windows that look out to a parking lot and a small grove of trees. The floor is cold and made of stone, and I shudder in the shadows as I realize that I am cold too. We are greeted by an older woman who identifies herself as a respiratory therapist. Her hair is gray, and her skin is creased and paper-thin. In a thick accent, she explains that she will need to take some bloodwork. As she pulls on your arm, I explain to her that you involuntarily flinch when your limbs are pulled and that it is very difficult to open up your arms for bloodwork. She nods and continues to pull. Every time she pulls, you pull back. Perspiration beads along her nose and forehead and I can see that she is struggling to hold the needle straight.

"Hold still! Can't you see I'm trying to get blood out!" she yells in your face, as she now violently pulls on your arm.

"That's enough!" My hands are shaking, and I feel the blood in my head pounding. "Can't you see that he is doing the best he can. I explained to you that he involuntarily pulls back when something tugs on his arm. How dare you scream in his face! Where is your compassion?" My voice is loud, and the small statured woman looks scared.

"I'm just trying to get blood out. I need to measure his oxygen levels."

"Then find another way!" I scream. She walks out of the room shaking her head. I draw my arms to my chest and stand over your bed, on guard. The nurse walks in and begins taking your vitals. I reported what happened, and she assures me that they will find another therapist. That first night, I stood on guard by your bedside. I didn't want to leave. I didn't know what was to come.

Your body was beginning to come alive. It started at the previous hospital and continued at this facility. At night, you began to writhe and scream and pull. Your arms and hands suddenly work, and it seems as if every nerve in your body is alive. Your arms flail about and you move from side to side. The staff placed a sign above your bed that has a cartoon of a huge face and eyes. Underneath the cartoon there are printed words that say, *Decannulation Risk*. It is meant to warn the staff that you might pull out your trach tube. They suggest restraints. This means tying your wrists to the bed. I refused them and said we would stand watch.

At night, the windows bring darkness and more cold into the room. There is an old heating and cooling box above the door. The nurses turn it to the coldest level to keep you cool. If the temperature in the room is above 60 degrees, you begin to sweat. I remind myself to bring a hat, jacket, and a blanket from home. It is now past midnight, and I pinch myself to keep from dosing off. A nursing assistant enters the room and introduces herself. She is all smiles and I can see that the despair and suffering of the hospital had not gotten to her.

"How ya doing?" She's talking to you as she works on getting you cleaned up and changed.

"Oh boy, you sure do move a lot. I know you wanna go home. I have no doubt about it. He's moving like he's fightin' for somethin'," She paused and looked up at me, as if seeing me for the first time. "Oh, you mus be da wife?" I nodded. "You got kids?" I answered that we have three boys. "Oh, now I know I wuz right. You fightin' to be home with dat beautiful woman and yo kids. I know you gonna be jus fine." She's talking to you as she works and lovingly pats your arm when she's finished. I feel the muscles in my arms begin to loosen at her voice. "Now you jus need to go home and get sum res . . . he's going to be jus fine." I give her a wan smile and feel my resolve beginning to melt. The thought of leaving you in this place makes me sick to my stomach. But I can't keep my eyes open much longer. "I promise you, we will take care of him. And, hon, I just know he's gonna be ok. Lookit how he move! He's a wantin' to get better. He gonna be home with his kids in no time. I just know these things." I wiped the tears burning in my eyes and forced a smile.

There were nights when we left you alone in that place and nights we stood watch. That nursing assistant was wonderful, but for all her cheer and happiness, there were ten more assistants that were overworked, overwhelmed, and unable to smile even once during their shift. There were rope burns on your wrists where the restraints were placed on too tight. There was an unexplained gash on your ankle. There was medication that was tapered too quickly. This mistake ultimately sent you into a full storm again. For several days, the storming returned. I felt as though I had failed you. I had failed to protect you. I felt immense guilt and shame for not being able to be by your side every second of every day. Doctors that are supposed to do no harm, made a huge mistake. Doctors that are supposed to have your best interests in mind failed to make the best decisions in your care. I became angry again. At God, at myself, and again at God for allowing this to happen. I remember driving to the hospital in the morning and hearing God's comforting words in my head that you will be healed, that everything will be ok.

"No!" I screamed. "I don't want to hear those words. I want you to heal him now. Fix this! Why did you ever let this happen? Why? Why? How could you? How?" I realized that I was screaming and crying out loud. I was at a stoplight and there was a man staring at me as I yelled. I didn't care. I kept screaming. It felt good to yell, to let it all out. It had become too much.

I had gotten a phone call that your storming had become so severe, they had to move you to the Intensive Care Unit because of your heart rate. My own heart hurt so much. I pulled up the drive to the large parking lot in front of the hospital. My stomach hurt as I saw the window to your room on the fourth floor. I opened the driver's side door to my car and swung my legs outside, catching my breath, and grasped the side of the car for support. *Be brave. Be a leader. You are all they have, Gabby. Your boys—all of them, Noah, Matthew, Nico—Arnoldo—they have you.* I took a deep breath and closed the door, grabbed my purse and a bag of snacks and water I brought to get me through the day. As I walked away from my car, a man stopped me. "Excuse me." His clothes were tattered and torn. They looked like they had not been washed in weeks. I immediately thought about the amount of money I had in my pocket, wondering if I had any dollar bills to give him. The parking lot was empty of people except for us, and I pulled my purse closer to my body. Standing up straight, I turned and faced him.

"Yes?" I was surprised at the impatience in my voice. I was tired, and suddenly, I felt the weight of the world and so much more upon my shoulders.

"Are you here to see someone?" he asked. His eyes looked warm underneath the ragged baseball cap on his head. His hair was disheveled, and tufts of brown and gray strands covered his ears.

"Yes," I answered, still wondering what he wanted. I held my purse taut as I stood facing him.

"I was here to see someone too—my sister." He paused for a second, not allowing me to answer. "Can I pray for you? I just feel as though I am supposed to ask."

This request completely surprised me. Here was a man that I expected was going to ask me for money, but instead was offering to give *me* something. I just nodded, feeling my body relax. He placed a strong hand on my shoulder. I noticed the way the skin on the back of his hand was bronzed by the sun. His fingernails were black and one finger on his hand was bandaged in gauze.

"Dear Lord, I stand here with your daughter and am praying for you to lift her up during this storm. Bring peace and healing to her and to her loved one. In Jesus' name, Amen." He smiled and turned to go.

"Thank you," I managed to say. He nodded and turned to go.

"Oh, I almost forgot. Here, please take this." He reached into his jacket pocket and handed me a small folded slip of paper. "Don't forget, he is always with you." I accepted the paper and looked down to read it. In large white font were the words *What a Friend we have in Jesus,* written against a backdrop of a meadow and mountains. I nodded to the man and walked away, wiping tears as I walked. Inside the folds of the paper was a poem. It read:

> *What a Friend we have in Jesus,*
>
> *All our sins and griefs to bear!*
>
> *What a privilege to carry*
>
> *Everything to God in prayer.*
>
> *O, what peace we often forfeit*
>
> *O, what needless pain we bear—*
>
> *All because we do not carry*
>
> *Everything to God in prayer*
>
> Joseph Scriven

It was God that had sent this message—of this I have no doubt. Again, in our darkest hours, he gently reminded me that he was with us—that we did not bear this pain alone. He was there to carry our burdens for us if we so chose. You, my sweet husband, were back in Intensive Care—suffering again. I was now ready for battle, with God at the helm of our army.

Had I not been reminded that Jesus was with us, I would not have been able to bear the sight of you in agony. I could hear your moans in the hallway before I reached your room. I entered the room and saw your body drenched in sweat. Your eyes were open and staring at the ceiling. One pupil was dilated and the other was not. Your teeth came over and bit your lip as your elbows buried themselves into the sides of the bed, causing you to moan and to lift your hips and writhe back and forth. Your fever was high, and your heartbeat had reached extremely high levels.

This continued for several days and several narcotic medications were introduced to calm your nervous system. After several days, the storm broke. A small victory—but a victory, nonetheless.

Your sister became my anchor during this time. I met with your doctors and case managers, and she met with them again on her own terms. I won't go into too much detail, but I can tell you that she made one of the doctors shake as she forced him to call the previous hospital and get more information about your medications. God gives us all gifts, and she was in her element in this place. Her strength helped me hold my ground as I stood up to the Case Manager, Director, and Customer Service Manager. I should have filed a lawsuit for the negligence in your care at this place. Yet, at the time, all I wanted was to focus on your healing. The energy I had was for YOU—to give to YOU and only YOU. I didn't want to focus on anything but that. Maybe I was wrong. Maybe I should have done more—especially as I think about future patients in this place. Yet, despite the poor quality of care, the dirty floors and loud sirens, you began to heal. Your trach tube was removed, and you began to speak. It was slow at first and words were garbled. Eventually you could say our names and speak some phrases on your own. Despite your eyes being open, we found that your vision was deeply affected. You could not see. Confusion set in and there were days when you would yell and swing at the nurses and staff. Other days, you would be still and sleep most of the day. Nights were always difficult. Your sleep was always minimal, and we began taking turns sleeping by your bedside at night to make sure you didn't hurt yourself.

Despite exhaustion, our hopes were high. Each day it would seem, you would reach a new milestone. A new phrase would be spoken, or you would laugh at something silly we said. Because of your known agitation with external noises and staff, you were given your own room. It was a tiny room at the end of the hallway. There was just enough room for a bed, a chair, sink, and small bathroom. The room had a large window that looked out onto the freeway and city below. When the window was open, a cool breeze filtered through the room, along with the roar of the freeway. If I closed my eyes, I envisioned we were in a private apartment overlooking the ocean. I could almost smell the salt in the air and feel the waves crashing over us.

I love you,

Gabby

SUPERMAN

"Rescue me, O Lord, from evil men; Preserve me from violent men . . ."

Psalm 140:1 (KJV)

San Jose, CA 1981

The late afternoon sunlight warmed the shady backyard of the stately old house. Two girls sit on the windy stone path giggling as they play. One has hair, dark as coal, that cascades down her back. It is usually combed in a thick braid, but today, it flows freely—locks covering her face, fair cheeks, and eyes as she moves. She is tall and thin and is clearly the older of the two. She is wearing a white and pink knit sweater with embroidered bears on the front. The other girl has shoulder-length cinnamon-colored hair that sits in wild ringlets around her face. The curls bounce as she moves, and she brushes them anxiously out of her eyes. This girl is short and small. Her legs are covered in mosquito bites, her knees slathered in bandages from a recent fall.

She is wearing a light blue, second-hand store dress and white leather shoes. She loathes dresses, but her mother is so insistent on them that she's given up complaining. St. Vincent de Paul is where most of them come from. If a dress is too long, or too big—her mom hems and alters them to fit. Once, her mother found a dark green dress and excitedly commented on the thickness of the material and the quality of the stitching. It was a perfect fit and needed no alterations. At $1.75, it was a bargain. She wore it that next Monday but had come home in tears. The children kept asking the girl what girl scout troop she belonged to, and she had realized with dismay that her new green dress was a Girl Scout Uniform. When she told her mom, her mom laughed and said, "Well, just tell them you *are* a girl scout!" The girl sobbed that she would never wear that dress again. Her mother didn't insist.

Today, she is playing in the backyard of an old house that her parents rent. To make some extra money, they also sublet several of the rooms in the house to other families. The tall girl with the long black hair belongs to one of those families. There is no doubt that the one hundred-year-old house was once a beautiful home. Large wooden steps lead to a stately porch that embraces the entire front of the house. Inside, there is a foyer, a parlor, former dining room, kitchen, large bedrooms, and a sun porch. The backyard has shady, windy stone paths, a koi pond, an outdoor stone and brick fireplace, a covered patio area, and a detached garage. Two double doors lead down to a damp, dark basement with dirt floors that run the length of the house. The girls avoided the basement. The dark, foreboding entrance was never an enticement for them in their play.

By the time the curly-haired girl's parents had moved into the house, the house was in major disrepair. The koi pond was filled with only rainwater and had been littered with dirt and debris. The trees and shrubs in the yard were overgrown and encroaching on the winding paths. Paint chipped from the outer walls of the house, and inside, the musty smell of moisture and dry rot filled some of the rooms. The house was sparsely furnished with mismatched garage-sale items. Nevertheless, the girl loved to play in the shade of the backyard—under the large redwood tree. When the family of the tall dark-haired girl moved in, she was happy to have found a playmate.

"Let's play house!" said the dark-haired girl.

"Ok, I'm married to Superman!" said the girl with the curly hair.

"Superman? Mmm ok, you are always married to him..." The other girl shrugged. "Fine, I'll marry Batman—." The girls laughed and played in the afternoon sun as they acted out their married life. The awkward curly-haired girl twirled around and around making her dress billow out in the cool afternoon air. She danced in this way around her make-believe house with her Superman.

February 2002

I'm frustrated. I had gone into the city for a job interview and could not find my way out. Arnoldo and I had been married for two months. We lived in San Bruno, CA, a foggy suburb outside San Francisco, in the backyard converted garage of a ranch house. He had already been there for several months as his job had promoted him into a sales job for a struggling office in that territory. I was just getting to know the area and having lived in small towns for the last twelve years, I was nervous about driving in the city. That morning, I had printed directions to my job interview, but had forgotten to print reverse directions. Where was the freeway? Frustrated, I pulled over on a side street and pulled out my flip-top cell phone.

"Hey, sweetie," Arnoldo's voice sounded rushed and distracted.

"Hey, sorry to bother you at work—I'm just wonderin' if you are near a computer and can MapQuest my location?"

"What?" He chuckled on the other end. "You lost?"

"No . . . I just don't know exactly where I am and can't find the freeway," I said reluctantly. I hated to give him ammunition for him to tease me about later. I would be hearing about this for years.

"So, you're lost."

"Yeah, I guess I am . . ." I said sheepishly.

"Ok, what street are you on?" I told him the street and cross street. "Let me see if I can find the address of one of these stores...hold on."

"No, it's ok—here let me explain how to get to the freeway. You got a pen?"

"Yeah . . ." I wrote down his directions—left at the stoplight, go down another mile, turn at the drugstore, right on the street with a large dog on the corner . . . He was teasing me.

"Arnoldo—I'm not in the mood for jokes." He laughed his large bellowing laugh.

"Look up. Now, look in your rear-view mirror." A blue-green sedan had pulled up behind me, and I could make out his dark hair. He stepped out of his car, still chuckling to himself. I got out of my car and we embraced.

"What are you doing here? How did you find me?"

"I was just down the street for a meeting, and I knew exactly where you were, but I just wanted to buy some time to get here." I hugged him and he bent down to kiss me—our lips met, and I could feel pulses of electricity running down my back and legs.

"Oh, man...wish I didn't have meetings this afternoon," he whispered. "I would take you home right now."

I leaned into his chest and pulled his body close to mine. "I love you, Superman," I whispered.

"Superman?"

"Yes, you are always rescuing me out of predicaments. I always wanted to marry Superman—just realizing I actually did." His strong arms squeezed me tight.

"Come—on, follow me, I'll lead you out to the freeway."

Dearest Nonè,

Many, many years ago, you wrote me an email. I've included it word for word below. I feel like it's a clue to a puzzle. Like you have been leaving me clues to decipher and this one is a huge one:

February 26, 2003

To: Gabriella Gannon

From: Arnoldo Avila

"Faith is the doorway that all miracles come through, but prayer is the key that unlocks the door"

I really like this quote. I generally do not appreciate these kinds of sappy emails, but I believe this simple quote holds a lot of value . . . . . .

Dear Nicholas,

Jesus loves you so much. Oh, my baby boy—you were so young when your father got sick, and it hurts my heart to know that you witnessed it—the cardiac arrest, the screams of your mother, the confusion and fear. I know that those things happened. I know that they are a part of you, but I pray that one day you will be able to see the beauty and miracles that have surrounded you. You and your brothers were not hurt. Angels came to distract you and play with you while your dad was being saved. You have grown in strength and understanding well beyond your years, my love. It will always be part of your story, but it will not be *your* story. From the moment you were conceived, your father and I knew you were special. You are so strong in mind and spirit. I know God has given you a fighting spirit for a reason. My baby boy—you will be four years old in

119

just a few months, and it pains me that you have not had your father healthy and well for half your life. However, you have remained strong in your faith and love. Every single night before bed, you pray—he is first in all your prayers. You love him so much, and he loves you. He is here for YOU and your brothers. I always wondered what your memories of your father are since all this happened when you were so young. I was so happy to hear you tell me that you remembered when he would hug you, when he would feed you, when he would put you to bed and tuck you in for the night. Those memories are exactly right. They are full of the love he has for you, my sweet boy.

I'll never forget the day you picked Superman as your costume for Halloween. You had never watched it on TV and never read about him. To you, he was an unknown, but you loved him. You wore that costume all year, and you wear that costume still. Somewhere, deep in your consciousness, you know that you and your dad are connected. For you see—Dada is Superman. He is Mommy's Superman. It's like you are standing in for him while Dada heals. It is unexplainable, but I do not question it. Every day, day in and day out, you wear your Superman costume to school, to the store, to church . . . Only God knows why you chose that superhero—why you love him, why you wear the costume— but for me, as I wait for your father to come home, seeing you gives me so much joy. It is as though God knew I needed a reminder that my Superman would be home and healed very soon. Nico, thank you for being you! Your fire will change the world. You have your father's strength and incredible energy and passion. I cannot wait to see how you will save the world, my little tiny Superman. God bless you always, my son.

Love, Mom

PRAYER OF POWER

"And whatever you ask in prayer, you will receive, if you have faith."

Matthew 21:22 (ESV)

San Leandro, CA – June 2017

Dear Arnoldo,

The dirt-tinged window is cracked open, and I can hear the low hum of the freeway fill your room. You are awake, and I call out your name as I walk in.

"Hi, sweetie," I said gently, and I smile to myself as you turn your head toward my voice. Your arms stretch out toward me. A new skill. Every day, we see new things happening with your body and I am filled with hope! The last time I visited, I had asked you about your car. It is a foreign car, and I had begun to drive it for the long drives to the hospital. On one of those trips, a light came on for service with a message that read, "Service A." I mentioned it to you, and you mouthed to me, "Oil Change." It was absolutely remarkable to see you remember small things and be able to communicate with us. Your voice would come and go, and sometimes, we would hear your words loud and clear; yet there were other days when they were mere whispers, or where you would mouth things with your lips. Today, your arms are outstretched, and this is amazing! We embrace and your eyes fill with tears. Mine burn with emotion too.

"Did you miss me?" I whispered into your neck. In response, I felt your arms squeeze me tighter. Your hands rubbed my back, legs, and arms. They were your eyes for now. Your vision was not back yet. Every day, we would ask if you could see us, if you could make out a certain color or shape or the number of fingers on our hands. Every day, your answer was no. You attempted to make room for me on the bed. That gesture was new too. I removed my jacket and scarf. Even though it is the middle of summer, everyone that comes to spend the night with you comes prepared with blankets, jackets, hoods and scarves. You have not learned to regulate your temperature yet and your body runs hot. Your room is always set to below 58 degrees.

"What shall we do?" you mouthed, and I kissed your cheek.

"What shall we do, my love? So much to talk about—so much to do!" Your arms outstretch and you pulled me close. I leaned into your chest and can hear the slowing of your heartbeat—the slow steady rhythm of your breathing and I knew you were asleep. My back ached, but I dared not move—I didn't want to wake you. The door creaked open and a nurse popped his head in, "Just checking in on him to make sure he's ok." I nodded. The door clicked closed and you awoke, your eyes wide, your arms flailing—I sat up. Your head moved from side to side, you were moaning, your hands reached for the leads attached to your chest and began yanking them off. I attempted to stop you and you pushed my hand away forcefully.

"Noni, it's me—it's Gabby, stop, sweetie, stop!" Your arms stopped fighting.

"Where are we?" you mouthed. "When do we go home? Where do we go from here?"

The anxiety and fear that gripped you was always there after waking up. It was as though in your sleep, something would re-set itself—something would change, and you would forget everything.

"It's Gabby, your wife—do you remember me?" Your hand squeezed mine in assurance.

"Good, you are in a hospital—getting better—do you remember why you are here?" Your hand wouldn't squeeze mine and I would tell you what happened. "We were driving—you were driving, and your heart went into a sudden cardiac arrest. You were in a coma, you woke up—you are healing..."

Often, this would calm you—the sound of my voice, the story, the reminder of what happened and why you were here. I reassured you that all was well—that you were healing, that the children were fine, that we are all just waiting for you to heal and come home. My heart would sink in these moments because I was instantly reminded that despite your gains and improvements, we had a long journey ahead of us.

During the calm times, when we had hours to talk, I would test your memory and ask you many questions. Did you know your birthdate, my birthdate, the names of your children, your favorite color, my favorite thing to do, etc. Talking was not easy, and you often would resort to hand squeezes for yes and no. I often listed the answers in multiple choice form, and you would squeeze my hand for the right answer. It was a long, painful method of communication, but it was communication nonetheless and it was incredibly reassuring to know that you knew yourself, you knew us, you had memories!

I could hear the siren-sounding alarms going off in unison down the hall in your unit. It was nearing bedtime and the nursing staff was changing shifts. Patients were asking for pain meds, help with bathroom care and maybe just comfort. So many of them were alone all day. You shifted nervously at the sound. I always wondered why they would have such horrible sounding alarms in a place that was meant for recovery—

especially for those with a brain injury. Peace and quiet was crucial for recovery. Your eyes were wide as we heard the sound of screaming down the hall. I patted your arm and reassured you that all was well.

"Where do we go from here?" you whispered to me. "I wanna go home." I saw your legs shift and you attempted to swing them over the bed. I needed to calm you before you had another anxiety attack.

"Baby, you remember where you are?" You squeezed my hand for yes. "Ok, let's remember that you are here to heal." You bucked your hips and I could tell that your anxiety was building. "Do you want to pray?"

"Yes," you whispered. We held hands and I said a prayer out loud. When I was finished, I looked over at you and asked you if you wanted to pray silently.

"Maybe God will give us guidance or answers as to why this happened."

You whispered, "Yes."

"Ok, close your eyes," I said. "Dear, Lord God, we are in a storm, and we know that in all your plans there is perfection. Today, we come before you to ask for guidance. Why did this happen? Is there a reason? What is the reason? Help us understand." We held hands with our eyes closed. My mind drifted and I strained to get it back into focus. *Why God, why did this happen?* I couldn't stop feeling angry and sad. I couldn't focus on hearing God. I opened my eyes and saw that you were sitting quietly with your eyes open.

"Did God talk to you? Did you get an answer?" My own mind had wandered so much that I felt disappointed at not being able to hear God.

"Yes," your voice cracked as you spoke.

"You did? That's wonderful! What did God say was the reason for this happening to you? To us? To our family?" You adjusted the blanket over your feet by bending your knees and pulling it up to your chin. It was a regular gesture—a gesture you had done hundreds of times at home and basically ever since I had met you. To an outside person it would have meant nothing, but to me it meant everything. It was normal and involved complex movements of your legs, arms, and feet. You had done that movement just a few days prior and it was exciting to see progress happening before our eyes.

"P...paa, paa... Prayer of Power." The words came out slowly and painstakingly, but loud and clear. *Prayer of Power?* I figured that perhaps your brain injury had caused you to jumble up words. That phrase didn't make much sense to me.

"Did you mean the Power of Prayer?" I offered. This would make sense as so many had gathered to continue praying for you—for us. You did not answer me. I asked again and looked at your face and hands to search for an answer. None came.

"Did you actually mean Prayer of Power?" I asked.

"Yes." You said quietly. It was clear that you knew the distinction between the two and that the words God had spoken were actually Prayer of Power. Your anxiety was gone, and you lay peacefully on the medical bed with your hands folded across your chest. *Prayer of Power?*

The next day, during my drive home, I phoned a friend and told her about the experience.

"No, I think he actually meant *Prayer of Power*. Gabby, think about those words and think about what that means." I sat in silence for a minute.

"I'm not sure..." I started and then my voice trailed off.

"It's a prayer said with such faith that it can move mountains. Gabby, the Lord is showing you and Arnoldo that what he's teaching you, and in turn all of us, is to pray with power. That we need PRAYERS OF POWER. I haven't said this to you before and I'm not sure how you will take it, but I feel sure that Arnoldo and your family was chosen. Arnoldo will come home fully healed. He will be fully restored, and his testimony will be incredible. You guys will travel and tell your story all over the world. I just know this."

Tears streamed down my cheeks, and I felt a knot in my stomach. I thanked her, and we hung up. So much to think about, Arnoldo. Her prophetic words were beautiful, and I prayed for them to come to pass. It wasn't the first time someone had said something similar to me. In fact, several people had said it—strangers, friends, family—but maybe somewhere deep inside I felt that they were just being nice—trying to lift me up under this dark storm. It wasn't until now, as I heard her speak, that I felt she may be right—that what they spoke was TRUTH. I am ready for that day.

Love, Gabby

HAVE FAITH

*"Now faith is the assurance of things hoped for,
the conviction of things not seen."*

(Hebrews 11:1)

June 2017

The luminous summer sky teamed with stars and I reveled in their beauty as I drove along the curved, one lane, country road. *Prayer of Power.* Arnoldo had given me something to think about. Well, God had. Something to contemplate and meditate on. The power of prayer is something I was familiar with—people prayed for each other and the more people that prayed the better. In his case, he had hundreds, if not thousands, praying throughout the country and the world. While this was important, this was NOT the message GOD had given Arnoldo. His message clearly stated, *Prayer of Power.* I looked to the Bible to help me find some meaning. *A prayer said with such faith that it can move mountains.* Faith. It wasn't enough to pray. It wasn't enough to cry out to God for help. Yes, this is crucial and an important aspect in our relationship and conversations with God, but God is asking us to go one step further. Faith. The Bible was full of instances where God asks us to *Have Faith.* Here are just a few examples:

Matthew 21:22
And whatever you ask in prayer, you will receive, if you have faith.

Romans 10:17
So faith comes from hearing, and hearing through the word of Christ.

Mark 11:22-24
And Jesus answered them, "Have faith in God. Truly, I say to you, whoever says to this mountain, 'Be taken up and thrown into the sea,' and does not doubt in his heart, but believes that what he says will come to pass, it will be done for him. Therefore I tell you, whatever you ask in prayer, believe that you have received it, and it will be yours.

1 Corinthians 2:5
That your faith might not rest in the wisdom of men but in the power of God.

Ephesians 2:8-9
For by grace you have been saved through faith. And this is not your own doing; it is the gift of God, not a result of works, so that no one may boast.

James 2:19
You believe that God is one; you do well. Even the demons believe—and shudder!

Luke 1:37
For nothing will be impossible with God.

Proverbs 3:5-6
Trust in the Lord with all your heart, and do not lean on your own understanding. In all your ways acknowledge him, and he will make straight your paths.

2 Corinthians 5:7
For we walk by faith, not by sight.

There are so many more. As I read these, I was reminded of the relationship between a parent and child. I imagined a young boy climbing on a jungle gym and getting stuck on the way to the top. When he yells, "Daddy—come help me," does he have any doubt that his father will help him? Does he think his father will ignore his cries? Or drop him to the ground? Or allow him to be hurt? No. He knows that his father will come and boost him up or guide him down. He JUST knows. Why? Because this father was there at his birth, held his hand when he took his first steps, guided him away from other dangerous situations, fed him, diapered him, clothed him, nurtured him, and over the years, this child knows that this man, who he just met a few years prior, loves him. The child does not question it. In his mind, he JUST KNOWS this. With all his heart he knows and trusts this man. And, so it is with God.

God has given us life, he clothes us with food and shelter and warmth, and when we find ourselves stuck on a tall jungle gym, he wants us to cry out to him with total faith, knowing He will be there to guide us—ready to catch us, lest we fall. So, when we cry out to him, our cries in prayer MUST be with the FULL and *complete belief* that he is there and will help us. Like a child believes, so must we. I should mention that sometimes a parent, who knows their child, will push him or her to learn. When a child cries, *Help Dad!* a father may respond by saying, *Keep climbing, don't be afraid, here—put one step up and then another!* Only a parent knows when a child might be ready. Only a parent knows when to push a child to grow and expand—yet that parent is there, ready to help, ready to catch the child if he should slip. It is the same with God. He may push our limits, he may ask us to go places we are not comfortable going, BUT he does this with the full knowledge that we are ready to grow. God will ask us to take another step knowing full well that we have the capability to reach the top of that jungle gym of life. He is always there, ready to guide us. He is our parent, our nurturer, our loving Father. He loves us.

I should stop here and say that I heard his message loud and clear. *Ask me for help but do so with the full faith and knowing that I will help you— Trust in me.* It sounded so easy—so simple—but in practice maybe not so easy. I wavered in my faith. I doubted. I argued and wallowed in my anger and fear. Let's not forget the *fear*. I was alone! A girl that had never been alone all her life. Arnoldo and I met when I was in my very early twenties. We had spent our entire youth together! Before that, I was in my parent's home and surrounded by their protection. I never learned to be alone, and when I was forced to lean on God, I realized I had never had to in the past. *To Fully Rely on Him.* Even then, when I doubted him, when I was angry, he was there—patiently waiting on me to hold his hand.

I was being told over and over by people from all different places that they felt certain Arnoldo was going to be fine. Not only would he be *healed*, but he and our family would travel the world to spread the message of God's love! These very words were spoken by many, and I have no doubt that God used them to remind me to focus on what was to come. They all would say this similar statement to me—that he would make a *full recovery*. The doctors have NEVER said that. They were simply amazed that he woke up and could sit up on his own or utter a word. They have continued to say that he will always have deficits, that he will never function the same, that he will not heal enough to be the father and husband that we need him to be—and yet, God has put it into the hearts of family, friends, and strangers to say out loud to me, *Oh, he's going to make a full recovery. I just KNOW he's going to be fine.* Don't forget that Mother Mary herself spoke these very words to me from the beginning. So where was my Faith? I was the child climbing the jungle gym—scared, alone, asking for help but not fully believing that help would come. I was that child trying to climb up on my own, angry and frustrated that I could not do it. God was giving me a hand, a boost, and I would slap his hand and scream *No!* and then cry when I couldn't do it on my own. Yet, our Father God is so gentle—so patient, and he gently guided me little by little to him in such a beautiful and loving way that there is no doubt he was there all along. He *never* left me. He will *never* leave you.

June 19, 2017

Dear Arnoldo,

Today, you took steps for the first time! Hallelujah! You walked! What joy! Your son Matthew was there and cheered you on! What a sight to see! My husband, standing tall on his own two feet! Thank God! You started swallowing and eating by mouth too! That makes me so happy! There have been beautiful miracles of our God in this horrible place. Just the other day, your speech therapist asked you when my birthday was, what the months of the year were, and the ages of your boys. She showed you techniques with your hands to push down, to get the words out. She's a tiny woman—small but loud and vibrant. She stood over your bed, hands on her tiny hips and she called your name. "Arnoldo—push—push those words out." You arched your back and pushed down with your hands and answered all her questions. She smiled from ear to ear—beaming with pride at your progress. We had become friends and she hugged me tight before leaving the room.

Despite your gains, the journey to your recovery lay before us—dark and unknown. There was the issue of the sudden cardiac arrest—why had it happened? Would it happen again? The doctors felt that you should have an implantable cardioverter defibrillator placed. They said the chances of another sudden cardiac arrest were high and that this would prevent your heart from stopping again. My stomach felt sick at the thought of having you come so far, to only lose you all over again. Yet, it was another procedure—an unknown.

At home, the boys were beginning to show signs of distress. Friends and family had helped up until now, but what they needed was both of their parents at home. At minimum, they needed one parent. They were acting out, testing boundaries, disobeying. I had received calls from neighbors about them being out in the street until late and about them being spotted at the community swimming pool without an adult present. The boys needed me and so did you. My heart was torn.

Your nights were still bad. Right around 11pm you would wake up in a panic, pulling on your leads, ripping them off your chest and legs, attempting to swing off the bed. Every night, it was the same. You were afraid, you screamed, you fought, and we stayed by your side. You slept off and on, two to three hours at a time. Your sisters, brothers, and I took turns taking on the nights. We calmed you—talked to you through the fear, we were there—voices of comfort and familiarity in your nightmare. At hearing our voices, you would begin to calm. Your heart rate would return to normal and you would return to sleep, only to wake again in two hours in the same panic. Lack of sleep begins to wear on the body. We began to grow weary. How long would this go on? When would this stop? One day, as night approached, my heart was heavy. I began to dread the nights as I knew the battle with your fears would begin. You squeezed my hand as I sat at your bedside. My worries overcame me. You have always had the uncanny ability to know what I was thinking—to know my feelings. There were times when I was home that I would suddenly be overcome with grief or sadness over the loss of my father, and you would call me from work. *What's wrong?* You would ask. You always knew. *Sweetie, I can feel you. You can't hide it from me. I can feel that something's wrong.* It was remarkable because you were never wrong.

Today was no exception. Your hand squeezed mine and your face looked worried. I couldn't hide my feelings from you, despite my attempts at small talk. I sat in silence at the edge of your bed. The reality of our situation began to come down on me—the fact that I had become a single parent overnight to three very small children—the fact that I needed to be your caregiver, but that I also needed to be there for our boys—the fact that your income was the only income, as I had been a stay at home mom for years. Questions like, *what am I going to do now?* Whirled in my head and the heaviness of it all sat on my heart.

Without meaning to, I said out loud, "What are we going to do? What are we going to do?" I regretted those words as soon as I said them. The last thing I wanted was to bring you more worry than what you were probably already feeling. You had stopped talking as much too. We had all noticed it. Today, you very intently sat up in bed. I helped straighten your robe. You squeezed my hand and then reached out to me—you were feeling for something. You placed your hand on my heart. Your lips pursed and I could tell you were attempting to say something. "B-b-be," you mouthed, "strong, h-have faith, everything will be ok." The words came out partly mouthed by your lips and partly whispered. Yet, they were clear. *Be strong, have faith, everything will be ok.* I said them out loud and you squeezed my hand in reassurance. Here you were, living your worst fear—trapped in your own body, laying in a hospital bed, frustrated and unable to respond, and yet you were giving *ME* comfort. But that has always been you, my love. Always putting others before yourself. My husband. My Superman.

Love,

Gabby

A PLACE OF MIRACLES

"I am the Lord, the God of all mankind. I there anything too hard for me?"

Jeremiah 32:27(NIV)

Arnoldo was moved to a rehabilitation hospital in the summer of 2017. He had been taking steps, swallowing ice, and relearning to talk. An ICD was placed in his heart in July and a few days later, he started rehabilitation. This was an exciting time for all of us. Arnoldo had survived the grimmest of situations and was now on the road to recovery. I don't know if all rehab places are the same, but the hospital Arnoldo was moved to was filled with the most loving and supportive staff we had met so far in our journey. By far, physical medicine and rehabilitation doctors are the most positive and encouraging physicians we had met on our journey. Therapy filled three hours of his day, and he began to learn to dress himself, sit on the edge of the bed by himself, stand and turn, take steps, swallow, feed himself, etc. Each day was filled with a new, small victory. He brought his spoon to his mouth. That was celebrated! For weeks, he would miss his mouth and hit his cheek or chin. He pulled on his pants by himself. He could remove his own shoes; he could assist in transferring himself from his bed to a wheelchair and back. All victories!

We tried to ignore the signs of decline. I mention this here because along with victories, there was also regression. He completely stopped speaking. It started slowly—as though his tongue began to stiffen and eventually, despite many attempts at saying words that had come easily to him before, he stopped trying. Swallowing became slower and more difficult and saliva pooled in his mouth where it had not before. We had been told from the beginning that recovery has many ups and downs and that this was normal, so I ignored this decline, even though my head was screaming with alarm.

There was an outdoor garden area that had become our special meeting place. The summers in San Jose are warm and mild and this garden provided shade and greenery. Trumpet flowers grew along a pergola and covered us in their fragrance as we sat outside. Birds visited the trees above us, and the warm sky blanketed us in its light. I loved this time outside with him, and I could tell he did too. One day as we were seated outside, I asked Arnoldo to say *I love you*. He tried to get the words out and found that his mouth was not working the way he wanted it too. His tongue stuck out and stiffened, and I could see in his face the frustration building.

"What is happening?" I asked him. "Tell me, is it your facial muscles that are not moving or your tongue?" I asked him to squeeze my hand for face and he didn't squeeze. He squeezed hard for tongue. "Is it completely stiff?" I asked. He squeezed hard for yes, and his eyes widened in terror. He was scared. "It's ok, my love. I'll chat with the doctors and find out what's happening." I was reassuring him, but inside I was scared too. I had already spoken to the doctors, and they did not have any idea why he would suddenly stop talking. "This does not generally happen," they explained. "We don't know what might have caused it." The unknown was dark and frightening. I tried my best to shield him from the uncertainty and kept encouraging him. Despite his speech completely leaving him, he was gaining strength in other areas and I focused on that.

July 20, 2017

I'm standing at Arnoldo's bedside. He's awake and the doctors are evaluating his G-tube site. The door opens and a thin tall woman comes in. She is elegantly dressed and has flowing black hair. She smiles. "Are you Arnoldo's wife?"

"Yes."

"Oh, I'm Casey Spencer, the case manager assigned to him. Nice to meet you. We haven't started to talk about his discharge, but I like to be prepared. Have you thought about what you are going to do? Will he go home?"

My gaze focused on her maroon lipstick and gold-rimmed glasses. Her perfectly manicured fingers tapped a black and white notebook impatiently.

"I...umm hadn't thought about it much. I mean, of course we want him to go home."

"Do you work?"

"No, I've been a stay at home mom—Arnoldo was our only income earner."

"Yeah, so what will you do? You have children?"

"Yes, we have three."

"Ages?"

I'm beginning to feel like I am being backed into a corner. "Ten, seven, and two," I answered. Her eyes widened.

"Oh, they are young—can you manage his care?"

"Well, not alone. I'm assuming I'll get caregivers to help." I wiped a small bead of perspiration off my temple. So many questions I had refused to think about. There hadn't been time. Each day was a fight to survive. "I'm sure we will figure things out." I stammered. I wasn't prepared to answer any of these questions.

"If you go back to work—which I'm assuming you will have to do, you will need help for him and will need to find childcare as well correct?" I nodded. "Can you afford that?"

"I don't know—I mean, what do people do in these situations?" I had no idea what to say.

"Well, people generally do different things—depends on the case. Looks like you have tried to apply for assistance and were denied." She looked at her watch and flashed me a smile. "You don't need to have all the answers now, but you need to start thinking about this. I have to run. I'll check back in soon. Bye!" She was gone. I looked down and saw Arnoldo laying motionless on the bed. He had heard her questions. He had heard my answers. She had spoken in front of him—as if he wasn't there. My heart pounded in rage. I loathed when people treated him like he did not exist or could not comprehend them. I was angry at myself for not asking her to leave.

"It's going to be ok, Nonè, don't listen to what she said. It will be fine. We got this. I PROMISE." I needed air. I needed to think and regroup. "I'll be back, babe—I'm going to grab some lunch." Arnoldo raised his arm in response. I stepped outside. Summers in San Jose are warm and beautiful. I have heard the region called *The Valley of the Heart's Delight* for its beauty and warmth. This was my hometown—our children's first town. I didn't know where to go, so I walked toward the parking lot and got into my car. I drove through the neighborhoods—thinking and asking, *God, what are we going to do? God, help us!* I heard a call coming in and resisted the urge to ignore it. I glanced at my phone and saw that it was Arnoldo's old boss.

"Hi, look, I just wanted to tell you that I looked into his retirement plan, and there is a disability component to it. This means that the money he set aside can be accessed for you guys—with no penalty. It will be as if he's fully vested. We can cut out the first check this week." He read off the amount. It was more than enough to live on for a while and hopefully pay for caregivers to help with Arnoldo's care at home. My eyes filled with tears. God was moving mountains. God was answering prayers. In our time of need, when we felt our most vulnerable, abandoned and empty, Jesus was right by our side. He had never left.

I needed to tell Arnoldo. He had overheard the entire conversation with the case manager and there was no doubt in my mind that he was worried and stressed. I drove directly back to the rehab hospital. Arnoldo was laying on his bed. His eyes closed and still. I could tell by his breathing that he wasn't asleep.

"Sweetie—hey—it's me," I whispered softly in his ear. I put my hand in his. "Are you awake?" His hand squeezed mine for yes. "Hey, how are you? I came back to tell you something . . ." He slowly turned his head toward me. "Do you remember when the case manager came in here and started asking me questions about taking you home and finances?" His hand gripped mine in a tight squeeze. I could see his eyes widen. He was definitely worried. "Guess what? I just got a call from your old boss. He told me there was a way for your retirement plan to be accessed—" I relayed all the details. "I wanted to tell you right away. I wasn't sure how much you heard of my conversation with that case manager lady. I wanted you to know that everything is going to be ok." Arnoldo burst into tears. Loud sobs filled the silence for a few minutes while I mopped away the tears from his cheeks and brushed my own away.

"Arnoldo, you were right, my love—you were right. God has us—he has THIS. Our only job is to walk in total faith. I'm trying to do what you said. You know . . . to *be strong, have faith and yes, everything will be ok.* I curled up next to him in a ball. He made no effort to hold me, move aside or offer any affection. We had all noticed that besides Arnoldo's speech, his body movements were getting slower, stiffer, and there was less initiation from him. The doctors had little to no explanation. We were *lucky,* they had said, that he did not end up like a pretzel. Apparently, most people with anoxic brain injuries as severe as his do. We were lucky that he was even doing what he was doing—that he was alive. I wanted to tell them that luck had nothing to do with it—that it was all God. Every ounce of this journey was God. Even when I doubted, even when I became angry or felt despair, God was gently reminding me, *I'm here. I never left; be strong, have faith, everything will be ok.*

THE EVERLASTING

*"So we make it our goal to please him, whether
we are at home in the body or away from it."*

2 Corinthians 5:9 (NIV)

San Jose, 2017

I was raised in San Jose and ultimately moved away when I was a freshman in high school. My parents relocated to a rural community in Northern California. It was a difficult move for me, and I never got over leaving my hometown. Once Arnoldo and I married, we lived in the San Francisco Bay Area and ultimately bought our first home in San Jose. We lived in that home for two years and made enough equity to purchase a larger home before the birth of our first child. The larger home was fine other than needing several cosmetic fixes. I quickly learned how much I loved remodeling, fixing, and making things *ours*. We spent countless hours agonizing over the type of flooring we would install, the paint colors, the tiles in the kitchen and bathrooms.

By this time in Arnoldo's career, his business had taken off, and we were doing well economically. I had a very good government job that brought us additional income. We both worked long hours, and I attended law school in the evenings. Our whole world was work, school, and material things. We bought new cars, new things for our new home and for ourselves. I consulted with decorators to help with each living space in our home and spent countless hours choosing pillows, accent rugs, curtains, etc. We went out to eat every night and on weekends we would fill our time visiting friends and family. I think back to this time and wonder where God was in our lives. Where was he in our hearts? We were not doing *bad things—we were not stealing or murdering or hating or lying—BUT, the truth was that we had put idols before God.*

Those idols were the material possessions we thought we needed to make us happy. Those idols were the houses, the décor, the trips, the cars, the clothes and purses and shoes—everything that defined our new world that was not God. It wasn't that we weren't grateful. We were. Both of us came from humble beginnings. My father was an artist at heart and worked blue-collar jobs all his life to provide for our family. His parents were immigrant farmworkers, and he grew up living in a small farm town with his siblings, while his parents worked the fields under the sweltering sun. We were definitely grateful. We had more money than we ever thought was possible. We gave money to our families and donated to charities. Yet, we often talked about how we needed to do more.

Deep down, we knew that this new lifestyle was missing something. Now, I know it was God. Our marriage was good, work was good, school was great. We felt happy—but not joyful. We had so much but felt empty. We were filling our time with anything but God. There was always that gnawing feeling that something was missing—that I was wasting valuable time and money on fleeting things. However, this message didn't really come into focus for me until that summer when Arnoldo was in San Jose at the rehab hospital.

We moved to Brentwood in 2010. It had been seven years since we had lived in San Jose. Being back was painful. Memories flooded my mind every day as I drove through familiar streets to the hospital. My dear friend, Deborah, had opened up her home to me during this time. She and her husband are a strong Christian couple. In fact, she probably does not know this, but years prior, she was the catalyst that brought me back to God. She worked as the secretary in the government office where I worked for many years. I remember how her entire face would light up as she spoke about Jesus and her entire church. Her spark ignited something in me that helped to bring me back to Christ, though it would be years later.

Staying in their home was a blessing for me during this time. They lived four miles from the hospital. Every night, they had a dinner ready for me when I returned home. We ate meals together and prayed together every day. Their home was filled with scripture. Every wall, mirror, counter, and corner were filled with scripture. Most of it was about *Faith*. I am sure that it was no accident that I ended up in their home during this time. My faith was being tested more than ever. Arnoldo had now stopped talking altogether. His tongue was stiffening every day. Saliva would pool in the corners of his mouth, and he was having difficulty swallowing. He was still eating pureed foods by mouth at this point, but his movements had become slower and slower. The hospital was pushing a fast discharge-to-home plan, and I was scrambling to get our home ready. My heart was heavy as I faced a huge unknown. Every day, on the mirror where I would comb my hair and get ready, I would see a small frame that read: *Now faith is the assurance of things hoped for, the conviction of things not seen. Hebrews 11:1* (ESV). It was a reminder to keep my faith, despite what I was seeing with my physical eyes.

In addition to the unknown fears and anxiety, my heart was in mourning. Being in San Jose was like pouring salt on a fresh wound. This was our city—where we shared the first decade of our marriage. Our relationship had grown here—our lives as one flesh. Everywhere I turned, a memory awaited me—stabbing my heart. Everything from the restaurant on the corner that we loved, libraries, parks where we had taken our first baby, to the spot where we had argued, and I had shared with him how much post-partum depression had affected me. Each was a painful landmark. Even streets would provoke pain as I remembered him sitting behind the wheel at a stoplight, chuckling out loud at some remark or observation I had made.

One evening, I left Arnoldo's bedside to find a new shower curtain for our downstairs shower. Arnoldo would be returning home soon, and I was making last-minute arrangements for his homecoming. I found myself in one of our old neighborhoods. The house we had lived in on this side of town was one we had remodeled from top to bottom. This was where we had spent countless hours carefully choosing hardwood, paint, and tile. I had spent many hours choosing furniture and accents and artwork. As I entered the shopping center, my heart and mind were flooded with memories. *Here is where we bought our lamps, where we shopped for the area rugs, where we bought our new baby's clothes, where we went to get the baby's bedroom furniture . . . .* Image after image flooded my mind of the two of us walking around stores and choosing things to buy. As I left the neighborhood, I felt a strong pull to drive by our old house. I did not want to drive by because I knew the memories would be so strong that I would break down. I kept driving, making my way back to the hospital. However, I heard God speak to me. *Go, drive by the old house.* The pull was so strong that I could not have stopped it, even if I wanted to.

Tears pooled in my eyes as I drove through the familiar neighborhood. The house looked the same from the outside. Tall cypress trees towered over the backyard and memories of laughter and family entered my mind. *Just wait—before you know it—Noah will be up there helping you trim those trees.* My mother in law's face beamed with pride as she had said this, pointing to an 8-month-old Noah who sat in his stroller, happily gurgling away. I remember how Arnoldo had laughed his loud boisterous laugh at how his mom was already putting our baby to work. It was hard to imagine our 8-month-old doing anything but eating and pooping. *It will be here before you know it.* Her face was joyful as she talked.

My plan was just to drive past the house, take a look, and head back to the hospital. As I drove past, I saw that the front door was slightly open. I parked the car and found myself walking up the driveway, pulled by an unseen force. I rang the doorbell and saws and hammering could be heard inside.

"Hello... hello?" I cracked open the door and poked my head inside. The house was empty of furniture and from the dust, it looked like it was in the middle of a full remodel. I looked around and gasped at the change. The hardwood floors that we had painstakingly anguished over were gone—ripped out and replaced by a contemporary vinyl. The classic lighting fixtures we had picked were all gone too. In their place were large white oval discs that spun together to make a contemporary statement piece. The house was completely different. This wasn't our home anymore. A man in overalls and a mask approached the door. Startled out of my thoughts, I stepped back. "Uh hi, are you the homeowner?" I managed to get out. The man shook his head.

"Owner not here," he answered in a thick Vietnamese accent.

"Oh, we used to own this house, and I just wanted to look inside—just to remember... Sorry, I didn't mean to intrude." The man shrugged. It was clear that he was a hired contractor and he looked anxious to get back to his work. He motioned for me to come inside. I stepped into the foyer and glanced around. Remnants of old memories still remained. The fireplace where baby Noah loved to crawl and sit, and the sliding glass doors covered by the blue canvas awnings still remained... Otherwise, the house was completely different. New, weathered gray vinyl floors flowed throughout, olive-green paint on the walls, white contemporary fixtures . . . all carefully chosen by someone else. This was someone else's home and new memories would be made for them. It was time for me to go.

As I drove away, I tried to understand what I was feeling. Was it sadness, disappointment, uneasiness? Tears flowed down my cheeks and

I couldn't stop sobbing. I pulled the car over and turned off the engine. Then I heard God speak to me. *Daughter, don't you see? Material things are fleeting—they come and go and change with time. It is the everlasting things that truly matter.*

In that moment, it all made sense. God had taken me back to a point in our lives where we had been filled with the desire to buy and fill our lives with material things. New furniture, new cars, new houses, new floors and tiles and area rugs—the list was endless. Yet, in an instant, it could, and would, all be gone. These were things of this world. I was shown that things of this world did not matter. Expensive floors ripped out. Countertops changed…an entire house gone. What things were left of that life? We had each other, the love we gave, the love of our first-born son, the love of family, the love of God. Those things remained and were everlasting. The rest did NOT matter. The message was clear. *Do not have any other Gods before me.* We had not worshiped Baal or Isis or any other foreign god. It had been our very own domestic god of material things—god of earthly possessions. We had spent so much time agonizing over every detail, and it was all gone. The only thing that remained was love. Love for each other, love for our children, love for truth and for God. I suddenly no longer felt anguish or fear. I felt so much love and gratitude for having been shown this beautiful lesson. God is love. Living in that love for each other is all that matters.

Those actions of selfless love—giving, helping, growing—are all part of our journey with God. Everything else serves as a distraction to keep us away from our one true purpose. I am not saying that we should all leave the cities and retreat into the forest to avoid material life—although many have done just that. That is NOT what I am saying. The lesson I learned that day is STOP. BE STILL. Look at where you are spending most of your time, energy, and focus. Is it on things of this world? Is it your career? Your house? Your appearance? Your success? Your worries and fears? Your past? Your future? Put God first. Spend time with him every day. Let HIM guide your every thought and action. Let go of what

146

was, what will be, and what could have been. With him at the center, focus on what to do for him and with him. These were the lessons I was learning. *Put God FIRST and focus on what is everlasting.*

When I returned to Arnoldo that night, I shared with him my experience. He listened intently as I described everything in detail, and I shared all that I had learned. He squeezed my hand in agreement. From that day forward, the debilitating pain I had felt at being in San Jose left me, and instead, I was filled with renewed FAITH. Instead of lamenting the past, I rejoiced that we were creating new memories. Memories of Arnoldo's illness, yes, but more importantly of recovery, of hope and healing—of life-changing miracles that would be everlasting.

HOME

"You are my refuge and my shield; I have put my hope in your word.'

Psalm 119:114 (NIV)

July 27, 2017

Dear Arnoldo,

A young man sat next to us at lunch today. He looked familiar and I recognized him from another hospital. He was on his own journey alongside of us. He too sat in a wheelchair and I saw that he was missing both of his legs from the knee down; his left arm was completely gone from the elbow down, and on his right hand he was missing all but two fingers. He nodded politely to us and I nodded back, focusing on helping you eat your lunch. You were learning to spoon feed yourself, and I was ready to make sure you didn't drip the food on your lap. We were celebrating the fact that you had been approved to eat pureed food by mouth for all your meals.

"I get to go home today," said the young man. I could tell he was contemplating something as he stared at his uneaten plate of food. "It's been nine months for me." I could tell that he needed to share his story.

"Nine months?" I nodded encouraging him to go on.

"Yes, I started feeling sick and thought I had the flu, and it turned out to be a serious brain infection. It spread to my blood, and by then, I was in a coma. The doctors had to amputate my legs and arm and part of my hand in order to save my life. I was in a coma for many months. I woke up and found that parts of my body were missing."

"But you are alive and going home today!" I said. Praying silently that I could offer words of comfort, knowing full well it was not up to me. It was his story, and he could see what happened to him as a tragedy or as a miracle.

"I'm so happy to be going home. I am a miracle," he whispered.

"Yes, yes you are!" I exclaimed with him. As he wheeled himself away and I sat there quietly in the warm patio area with you, I felt the intensity of this place. They all were miracles. Every single patient was a survivor—they each had their own miraculous story of overcoming death. For whatever reason, God had intended them to remain alive, and they were all here, striving to improve and get better. You too, my love, you too are a miracle.

By now, we had been here for several weeks, and we had gotten to know many of the patients and their families. There was the young newly-wed who had gotten in a motorcycle accident, the man who had fallen off a roof and hit his head, there were golf cart accidents, car accidents, stroke victims—all a unique story of what led them to be at this place of new beginnings. Despite their differences, they all had one thing in common. They had survived the ICU and were alive. Each person was a walking miracle. Each person carried their own story of perseverance, strength, and God's grace. Lives all changed forever, in an instant. I sometimes imagined each patient in his previous life—businessmen, construction workers, mothers, fathers, students, grandmothers and grandfathers. What would happen to them now? Who would care for them? Would it take years or months? What about you? What about us? I pushed these thoughts away and focused on the day to day. God had to guide us through. What other choice did we have?

Love,
Gabby

Arnoldo came home on August 17, 2017. Most people do not know that this date is *also* our Wedding Anniversary. Arnoldo and I were married in Guadalajara, Jalisco, Mexico on December 29, 2001. We married in the same colonial church my parents were married in years before. Because our wedding was international, we decided that we wanted to complete our civil marriage in the United States. We had a private civil marriage in the City Hall of San Francisco, on August 17, 2001—the summer before our *real* wedding in Guadalajara. We were alone—no rings, no witnesses—just a quick exchange of vows before a judge and signatures. It was meant to be civil and legal. We never celebrated this date or even considered it our wedding date. Our wedding anniversary was December 29th —the day we proclaimed our love and vows to care for one another in sickness and in health before God and all our loved ones.

However, I felt it was not a coincidence that his coming home day was August 17th. God had shown me so many little signs of him being there, in so many ways—letting us know that he is always with us. The fact that this date was picked was not a coincidence. I knew this in my heart. Just a few days prior, I spent a Sunday with Arnoldo going to church. The rehab hospital liked to have patients do small permitted outings with family as a step before going home. As we walked into the church, the choir was singing, *How Can I Keep From Singing*. This song was my father's favorite hymn. I felt as though the Lord was showing us that we were not alone. Arnoldo burst into tears upon hearing it. He knew what that message meant too. God was with us. Our journey had taken a new turn, but God was always there to hold our hand.

Dear Arnoldo,

It is 9 pm and the boys are tucked into bed. My eyes are heavy, and I snuggled my body into the couch, knowing that I have only a few hours before I need to be up. I drift off into a dreamless sleep. The muffled sound of gasping and crying startles me awake. My heart is pounding, and I leap up. I can hear the muffled sounds of someone talking and then the sounds get louder and louder. I pull on my robe and walk toward your room. The clock on the kitchen wall says it's 11 pm— we call it the witching hour. I open the door and see that you are sitting on the edge of the bed. Your body is covered in sweat. Your eyes are wide, and you are pointing to the wall. Your caregiver, a small thin young man with a gentle smile is sitting beside you, holding your hand. Your face changes to a look of horror and the screaming begins, again.

"Nonè," I say calmly. "It's me, Gabby—you are safe, you are home now. There is nothing to fear." At the sound of my voice, you are comforted. I put your hand in mine, and I feel you squeeze.

"It's ok," I tell the caregiver. "I'll stay with him—you go sleep on the couch." He nods, his eyes look red and tired. We get you settled back into bed, and I snuggle next to you. The hospital released you to go home and encouraged us to integrate you into an environment that would encourage healing. Other than bars on the side of the bed, nothing much has changed in the room. You are able to do so much these days. You can swing your legs over and sit on the side of the bed with minimal assistance; you can stand and turn and pivot to help get you in and out of your wheelchair. You walk with a walker around the house, all your meals are given by mouth now, and the only substances that go through your G-Tube are water and medication. You are more awake during the day as well. Nights, however, have remained the same. Every hour or two, you awaken, frightened, and you scream and fight invisible demons, until you hear the sound of my voice lulling you back to sleep.

By morning, I am bone tired. I can hear Nico screaming for me in his crib by 6:30am. This was the pattern of our new life. Dad was home, but things are so different. The caregivers are helpful, but their level of knowledge about brain injuries is slim to none. We are all learning. Your own patience is non-existent. As you integrate back into the household, you discover that you are not able to do what you are used to doing. You cannot get out of bed on your own or use the bathroom on your own. Meals are always with assistance and taking steps are done with a walker and the help of a caregiver. If you failed to maneuver the walker, or could not take additional steps, you scream and yell. It was frightening for the children to see their father this way. It is difficult for them to understand that YES, their father is home, but he is not the same—not yet.

October 2017

Dear God,

Arnoldo has been home for several months. The world around us assumes that we must be rejoicing—that things must be settled into our "new normal." They don't understand. They cannot even imagine our struggles. I know I couldn't if I were them. Only someone walking this path would get it. God, help us. Arnoldo does not sleep—he wakes every hour, and I am there to assist the caregiver in stretching him, moving him, and standing him up. During the day, he sleeps slightly more, but the boys need me. There are school pickups, drop-offs, homework questions, meals, bedtime routine, snuggle time with mom. I feel like everyone needs a piece of me, and I don't have anything else to give. I wish I could tear myself up into little tiny pieces and disperse myself to all that need me. I have not slept in months, and the fatigue is wearing on me. I lose my temper easily. I snap at the children. I am frustrated easily, and I feel immense guilt at not being better. I need to be a better mother, a better wife, a better caregiver. I feel guilt when I sleep, and the caregivers are left alone with Arnoldo. I feel guilt for them and for him. I feel guilt when I don't sleep and cannot be whole for our family. Two nights ago, I was driving to the store with Matthew. I forgot my purse and ran into the house to grab it, leaving Matthew in the parked car in our garage.

"Mommy, mommy!" I heard his screams inside the house, and I ran back out to the garage only to see my car slowly rolling down the driveway. Matthew had jumped out of the moving car and was standing inches from the tires. I ran and leapt into the driver's seat and hit the brakes. Matthew was white and shaking. I was shaking too. In my haste, in my own exhaustion, I had forgotten to put the car in park and had accidentally left it in neutral. I shuddered at the thought of what *could* have happened. You sent your angels to protect him, Lord. Thank you. God, please protect our family. I need to rest to be better. I need to sleep, to allow me to be the best mother and wife I can be.

I trust in you Lord—help us,

Gabby

October 2017

"Arnoldo, Arnoldo—what is wrong? Take a deep breath, put your hands on your chest, and close your eyes. You are safe. It is time for sleep now." He relaxed his arms and closed his eyes. The muscles in his face relaxed, and I could see the steady rhythm of his face as sleep overcame him. It was 2 am and his sleep patterns were becoming more and more erratic. I felt my eyes grow heavy, but I fought the urge to sleep. I didn't like the feeling of being startled awake and preferred to stay awake. Sure enough, less than twenty minutes later, I heard Arnoldo groan. His legs stiffened, his head tilted back, eyes shut tight, heavy breathing and a high-pitched moan escaped his lips.

"Arnoldo, it's me—it's Gabby. You are safe. Take a deep breath." This time my voice had no effect. His legs lifted up straight, as his back arched.

The entire weight of his body was now on his tailbone. His screams filled the night air, and the caregiver came running in with a groggy look on his face.

"Help me stand him," I commanded. We each grabbed an arm and sat him up. His body was stiff. Every ounce of muscle contracted into cemented brick mortar. His tongue curled up into his mouth and reminded me of the way a newborn infant's tongue curled during a colicky crying fit. We helped Arnoldo to his feet, and his back stayed stiff and bent.

"Straighten your back," I commanded, afraid that he would fall forward, and I would not have the strength to catch him. On his feet, his body was beginning to relax, and I felt his muscles ease. We turned his body and helped to get him into his wheelchair. Once in his chair, he took deep breaths. His body relaxed, and we began mopping his face with a clean towel. Sweat dripped down his neck and back. I rinsed the cloth with warm water and cleaned his body, face, and hair. What is happening, God? These were new seizure-like episodes. They were happening more and more frequently and had become more frequent and more intense. The nights were the worst. Two days of hospitalization and testing had determined that these episodes were not seizures. They did not know exactly what they were but called them muscle spasms and sent him home with medication that did not work. We were on our own.

Fall is in the air. The leaves are turning into their colorful hues of reds, golds, and oranges. Halloween is near, and Noah is ecstatic. It's his favorite holiday. He loves everything about it.

"Hey, sweetie, good morning." It is Saturday morning, and Noah has slept most of the morning. "Time to get up."

"Hi, mom," he gives me a half smile through sleepy eyes. When did he start calling me mom? It sounds so grown up. I miss the days of *mama* and *mommy*.

"How did you sleep?" I ask, dreading the answer. He hesitates.

"Ok, I guess." I know why he's hesitating. We all have been trying to carry on as normal, but the unspoken is heavy.

"Did you hear a lot last night?" I ask quietly.

"Yeah, but I just cover my ears—it's ok, mom." My 10-year-old pats my arm. He's comforting me. Arnoldo's screams at night have become normal somehow. In the darkness, they pierce the stillness of the night. I've talked to the boys about it. We've talked about how he's unable to communicate and how screaming is his only way. I don't tell them about the pain he must be feeling or the intense fear and anger at being trapped in a body that doesn't respond as he wishes. I don't tell them about the pain and anguish I feel at seeing their faces, pale with fear and apprehension, while their father screams in agony. I don't tell them that this is the absolute LAST thing their father would want them to witness. Arnoldo, my Superman, our protector. I know in my heart that Arnoldo cannot possibly help himself and he cannot possibly stop the screaming, because if he could, he would. He has always been such a huge protector of our family. How could this not be hurting him or affecting him? I pictured our little boys in their beds at night, awakened by the screams—the sounds of muffled voices coming through the walls as the caregiver and I attempt to help. The feeling of fear and helplessness overcoming them as they see their hero, the leader of our pack, the strongest man they know, now completely helpless and in agony.

I try my best to do weekend meals as a family. My mom and aunt bustle about the kitchen, and the boys are seated at the table. I call the caregiver to bring Arnoldo to the table for breakfast. It is important to me that we eat together. It is a small shred of normalcy. As Arnoldo is wheeled to the table, his hands and arms stiffen, his legs extend and his back arches. *Oh no, it's a spasm.* His head tilts back and his eyes are tightly shut.

"Breathe, Arnoldo, breathe. Take deep breaths," I command. I can often guide him through the seizures and help keep them from getting worse. His head tilts back and his mouth parts open. I can see that his tongue is curled up against the roof of his mouth. The caregiver massages his calves and feet. It is all to no avail. The spasm hits and his face and neck break out in beads of sweat. The scream leaves his lips and his body convulses. Noah and Matthew look down at their food and continue eating. This isn't a new occurrence. Nico has left his seat and runs over to his father's lap. He places his small hands on his leg. "Is ok, Dada—you ok," he says, patting him as he talks. Arnoldo's body twists and turns, and the screams continue.

"Why Dada crying?" he asks, his chubby, rosy face clouded in concern. His chocolate eyes are wide and glistening.

"It's ok, Nico. It's ok—Dada just needs to stand up—it's ok." I motion to the caregiver to take him back to his room, and I follow, leaving the boys alone to finish eating.

"Mommy, mommy, mommy!" screams my youngest boy. He's still a baby. He doesn't understand any of this.

"It's ok, just go eat your food," I whisper. "I'll be right back. My voice is quiet, and my body is weary.

"Don't go," he cries. "Why is Dada crying?" As I walked away, I heard his footsteps behind me. I didn't have the energy to stop him. The caregiver and I stand on each side of Arnoldo and hoist him to his feet. This was the only way to stop the spasms in their tracks. Nico stands behind his wheelchair. "Good job, Dada—is ok—you ok." His chubby hands clap together as he comforts his father. I feel my eyes fill with burning tears, but I choke them back down. *Don't cry, don't scare the baby more than he's already scared.* My little, tiny Superman—helping his big Superman feel better.

November 2017

Every day, the muscle spasms became more frequent and more intense. I phoned every doctor, pharmacist, and nurse I knew. His general physician did not know what to do and suggested he be seen by his neurologist. The neuro team recommended raising his dose of meds and referred him back to his general physician. They stopped returning my calls after a while. Emails went unanswered or were vague. Meanwhile, his body became rigid, stiff, and cement-like. His limbs hardened, and his hands and fingers closed tight in a fist. Every night, Arnoldo would scream in agony, and the caregiver and I would work to change his position, stand him up, and try to help.

By early December, the spasms were continuous. They were so bad that he was unable to eat. I called an ambulance when his body stiffened for so long that he was no longer able to sit in his wheelchair. He was taken to one of the better nearby hospitals. After being there for only 24 hours, the doctors pulled me aside and asked me why hadn't I taken him back to the previous hospital. They did not feel confident that they could do much for him at this hospital, except keep him comfortable. I was at a loss. I had not slept in months, and my own body was starting to show signs of distress. My once full hair had now fallen out and was half the volume it once was; I had lost a significant amount of weight, and I know my weariness and stress showed in my face. They moved Arnoldo to ICU and put him on heavy opioid medications. The spasms would slow, but once the medication wore off, they would return. After one week in ICU, one of the doctors pulled me aside and said, "There's nothing more we can do for him here. We don't have the knowledge or expertise." My eyes burned with frustration. *How could they not know what to do? They were doctors! What could I do?* I began battling with the insurance to get him transferred to the best academic teaching hospitals in our area. Both transfers were quickly declined. This felt all too familiar. We were stuck. I paced the halls, praying for a miracle and asking God to show me the way. Two days later, one of the doctors in his unit pulled me aside.

"If it were my family, I would take him out of here myself and drive him to the emergency department of the hospital you want him to go. There's no other way. I'll never publicly admit to this—but there isn't another way. Officially, on record, I am going to tell you that taking him out of our ICU is going against medical advice. Do you understand what I'm saying?" She looked at me intently, and I nodded. I knew exactly what I had to do. The choice was clear. To leave him at this hospital would be to sign his death sentence. They would keep him sedated and allow his body to waste away. His blood pressure was dangerously low, his heart rate was also very low, due to the drugs he was taking. Leave him there to die? Or fight. It wasn't a choice. He needed care—better care—and I had to fight . . . again. We had come so far—I couldn't give up now.

"Hey there—I need your help." I had called his youngest brother.

"What's going on?" he asked.

"I'm moving him out of here tonight, and I will need your help to get him in my car."

"They approved the transfer?"

"No, that's why we are moving him." I described my plan. I could tell he was reluctant.

"I'm doing it with or without your help, we need to save him."

"When?" he asked.

"Tonight—we can't wait."

"Ok," he agreed.

That night, I told the doctors that I was taking him out of the hospital. They advised against it. I insisted. The nursing staff placed him in a chair for me. He was heavily medicated and unable to hold his own head up. As one of the doctors handed me forms to sign, she stated, "We are not allowed to help you load him in your car." I nodded. I figured as much.

Once he was safely in his chair, I pushed him down the hallway toward the elevator. His brother walked by his side to make sure he didn't fall.

"I'm going on my break," I overheard one of the nurses say. She caught up to us in the elevator. "I'm on my break—I'll help you load him in the car." Her sandy hair glistened in the fluorescent light.

"Are you sure?" I asked. I didn't want her to get fired.

"Absolutely. What I do on my break is my business." I could see the concern in her eyes. There are people who go into nursing because of their love for helping other people against all odds. Their purpose breaks free of any constraints imposed by outside factors. She was one of them. I envisioned her tending to bloody soldiers along the front lines of battle.

My car was parked along the curb of the entrance to the hospital. Between the three of us, we got him inside. We reclined the seat and laid him back. It was done and we were off. We headed back to the previous hospital. They had saved his life before, and they could do it again.

There were crowds of people in emergency that night. The dilapidated chairs lined the waiting room, and the cries of children were only muffled by the sounds of constant coughing. Arnoldo lay sleeping in his chair. He looked comfortable. After several minutes, a distracted nurse motioned us back for the initial intake. I maneuvered him through a brightly lit hallway. Gurneys lined the walls, each filled with a patient.

"We are super full tonight," he explained, waving his hand toward the gurneys. He opened the door to a corner room that looked like it might have once been a supply closet. Arnoldo was laid out on a bed, clothed with a robe, and vitals were taken. The nurse asked the reason for our visit. I described the spasms and the nurse looked doubtfully over at him.

"Yeah, I'm not sure what we can do here in the ER. He looks pretty comfortable. We are probably just going to send him home and have you make an appointment." Arnoldo had his eyes closed and looked to be in a deep sleep. The nurse walked out of the room, and Arnoldo and I were alone. I want to write that, at this point, I closed my eyes and prayed—that I got on my knees and called upon Jesus to help—but that would be untrue. Despite everything God had shown me to this point, I was STILL relying on myself. I was STILL relying on my own human knowledge—my own understanding and logic. Yet, looking back, Jesus had never left my side. In fact, he was holding my hand—I just did not know it.

An hour went by and Arnoldo began to stir—sweat pooled around his forehead—the spasms were returning. His head tilted back, his back arched, his legs stiffened, and he screamed—and screamed and screamed. The same distracted nurse popped his head in.

"Everything ok?" he asked.

"No, he's in pain. He's having spasms." The nurse left and came back moments later with a young bearded man that looked to be in his early thirties. He introduced himself as Dr. Smith. He asked several questions and took a look at Arnoldo's vitals.

"We are going to take him into a private room, so our neurologist can see him in the morning. There is no guarantee that he will be admitted."

"Well, then, you will have to figure out where to take him because I am not taking him home. It's not safe," I countered back. He frowned and stepped out of the room. I knew the game. They had seen Arnoldo's charts and knew the extent of his injury. They wanted me to manage him at home because they didn't know what to do. Sure enough, he was eventually admitted, and his condition stumped the medical neuro team. They tried various types of medication, but none made significant changes. Meanwhile, the spasms continued, over and over—he was screaming, sweating, and his weight continued to drop. Several teams of neurologists rounded daily—each hoping for improvement. After only three days, one of the attending doctors came to see him with his team of residents. After going through the typical presentation of symptoms and procedures, he announced that he was planning to discharge him by the end of the week. I have no doubt that God gave me the courage and the words to say what came out of my mouth next.

"Where do you plan on sending him?"

"To a Skilled Nursing Facility."

"Have you found the cause and remedy for his spasms?" I pointed to Arnoldo, who was still writhing in pain.

"No—err," he cleared his throat. "The medications we have used have not had any effect."

"If a patient comes to you with a broken leg, do you discharge him without fixing the break?" I asked, staring at his small black eyes.

"What? Err, no . . ."

"Well, we have come to one of the top hospitals in the country with a medical issue. You are telling me you either don't know, OR are not interested in fixing the issue and instead are recommending that he be sent to a lower level of care, where they will not only NOT know what to do, but will more than likely call 911, and he will end up right back in your ER and repeat this cycle again. Do you really want to be responsible for putting him through that distress, OR do you want to be part of the solution?" The balding, beady-eyed doctor stared intently at my face for a moment in silence. The room was full of residents and nurses. He cleared his throat.

"Well, let me see if we can have another specialist from our movement disorder clinic take a look."

Ultimately, it wasn't their neurologist that helped Arnoldo, but one of my favorite types of doctors! A Physical Medicine and Rehabilitation doctor had come by to evaluate him, to see if he might benefit from therapy. "Oh, he's storming," she declared, taking one look at him. "He needs beta blockers." This made sense. He had all the symptoms of storming—the sweating, the movements, high heart rate, weight loss.

Storming so late past the injury was very rare—but it was the only thing that made sense. I asked her to order the beta blockers, but she had to go through his neuro-team, and they declined her request. I was furious. Another battle. Only God could have been holding me up at this point. I called a meeting with his neurologists and outlined all the medication they had tried and had failed to work. In my heart, I knew it was an ego-thing. A doctor from outside their group had dared to suggest something they hadn't thought of themselves. We didn't have time to tiptoe around egos and feelings. Arnoldo's life was on the line. I demanded they try her suggestion, and they reluctantly agreed. By now, Arnoldo had lost another seven pounds. He looked emaciated—cheek bones protruding, hip bones and ribs showing. They tried a small dose of beta-blockers, and the spasms decreased immediately.

It was a small victory, but the storm wasn't over just yet. As soon as his symptoms became more manageable, the hospital pushed for immediate discharge. He was not ready for home, so we pushed for him to go back to a rehabilitation center as opposed to a skilled nursing center. Within a few days, he was back at the same rehabilitation facility he had gone to several months prior. The staff remembered him and welcomed him back. I could see the genuine concern on their faces as they saw how thin and sick he was. His spasms continued, although the medication had helped to control them. The new medicine caused his blood pressure to drop, but he would spasm continuously without it. He was given a different medicine to raise his blood pressure, so that the beta blockers would not cause his blood pressure to drop to a dangerously low level. It was a circus. His blood pressure went up and down erratically. His body needed the right dose—some days were good, and others were terrible. He couldn't hold his own head up, let alone participate in therapy. By the end of the month, the hospital stopped giving him therapy. *He was unable to make gains. Unable to participate. His health was never consistent. He was too weak. Too tired.* Goodness, the man had just stormed for over 30 days. He had lost 85 pounds and was a shadow of himself. What he needed was time. In my heart, I knew this. Time. I was going to give him that time.

ONE YEAR LATER

*"He has made everything beautiful in its time.
He has also set eternity in the human heart; yet no one can fathom what God
has done from beginning to end."*

Ecclesiastes 3:11 (NIV)

Sunday, March 25, 2018

Today is Palm Sunday. It is the day that commemorates Jesus' triumphant entry into Jerusalem. It is the day marking the beginning of Holy Week, and as a dear friend phrased it, "it is a very significant day of Jesus entering his phase of knowing what was ahead."

On this beautiful sunny Palm Sunday, exactly one year ago, our beloved Arnoldo, my loving husband, amazing father to three boys, brother, son, and friend to many, entered into the shadows of human suffering— into the pain and agony of near death, the trials of attempting to recover what was lost. He and all of us that love him entered into this shadow with him. Here we have remained, only surviving through prayer, meditation, hope, and most importantly, FAITH.

For one year, Arnoldo has struggled with the physical and has heard his beloved family suffering with him. YET, there is one constant that has remained strong in him for that year; one element that has never wavered, that he has never questioned, not once, not ever, and that is his full and complete FAITH in God. During the early days when Arnoldo was just coming out of his coma and began to talk, the words that stand out most to me are the following: "Be strong, have faith, everything will be ok." Here he was in a hospital bed, recovering from a devastating injury, and he was comforting me! He was sharing his deep faith in God that gave him the strength to continue his journey. Arnoldo subsequently lost his ability to speak and remained silent for many months. This past November, during a particularly difficult day, he heard me crying out to God for answers. Through what I can only assume was the Holy Spirit, he began to speak again, for just a moment, and said to me, "Have faith."

Today, we are at the eve of the most important week of the Christian calendar. Today marks our entry into Holy Week, and God is asking us to do the same: "Have faith." All of us carry sorrow and suffering in our hearts. It may be the loss of a loved one, a health condition, a difficult marriage, the agony of seeing our parents become sick and elderly, a sick child, fear, anxiety, anger, guilt . . . it doesn't matter WHAT IT is. Jesus knows our pain. He knows our sorrow and knows exactly what is in our hearts. He also carries us in his heart, and he wants us to know that "everything is going to be ok." It really is! We are mere travelers to this earth…a short journey… and HOME is coming sooner than we can fathom. So WHY? Why all the pain? Why the suffering? Why are we here? What is being asked of us? Every time I ask these questions, the answer I receive is "TO LOVE." GOD is simply LOVE. It is not any more complicated than that. He asks us to act in love, to think in love in EVERYTHING we do. If we are true to this, then we are walking with him, through him, for him.

During the most difficult year of our lives, our family saw an entire community come together in LOVE for us. Through our sorrow, those around us became the hands and feet of Christ. People we both knew and people we had never before met, came together to bring us meals, donate money, and care for our children. Most importantly, these people came together in prayer and in FAITH.

Everyone that has ever met Arnoldo praised his love—his love for family, his love for his friends and community, his selflessness. Love was met with even more love. As Arnoldo healed, people have filled us with selfless love and reminders of FAITH. Over the past year, Arnoldo began to beat all the odds. He was never supposed to wake up—he did. He was never supposed to know us—he does. He was never supposed to be able to sit by himself—he does. He was never supposed to speak—he did. The miracles started at the very beginning—from the day of his accident. From the woman and doctor on the freeway that saved his life—to the mysterious man with flares guiding traffic around our vehicle—to the miraculous recovery. His journey has not been easy. Recovery has been met with setbacks, regressions, physical difficulties—he is not fully healed, but he believes, and I believe, that FULL healing is coming. And when it does, it will be to give full glory to the one and only God Almighty. God has remained by our side—despite my anger, my agony, my questioning— He was there—a constant in this journey of faith. I in no way believe that this happening on Palm Sunday was a coincidence. It is meant to parallel Christ's journey…just as ALL our lives are meant to parallel his journey.

We suffer in the shadows to be able to bask in his light! Today, on Palm Sunday, I reflect back on the idea that one year ago, we were entering the shadows… and that our faith would be tested, and our love would be tested. What has happened for a year has not been easy, but I know that God's miracles have guided us along the way. I have been reminded of our soul journey that involved so many others. I have been made aware that many came to God through our journey! We look forward to bringing many more to him as we continue on our path. I am honored by this opportunity, and I am grateful for all of you that have answered his calling and have kept us in prayer. Today, I offer my prayers and FAITH for all of you and your suffering. I pray that you remain strong, that you do NOT WAVER, that you remember who you are, and that you always remain "strong, have faith, and know that everything will be OK," no matter what.

May 2018

The footsteps at the door sounded unfamiliar. I turned to see who was walking into his room. Five months had passed since Arnoldo's admittance back to the rehab hospital. His expensive, top of the line insurance, which I had been covering on my own, had stopped paying for his stay. They had argued that he did not need to be in a hospital any longer and needed to be sent to another facility. All other facilities declined him. We were stuck. I could not safely take him home, and I could not find a place for him that would accept him. I did not share any of this with Arnoldo. I knew too well how deeply he was affected by hearing news that he had no control over and no ability to solve. The hospital case manager had already called my phone several times. There was no point in avoiding her—the curtain around Arnoldo's bed was drawn and I could see the tips of her black heels.

"Hello?" Her nasal voice echoed in his room.

"Hi."

"Oh, I'm glad I caught you. I want to discuss some things with you."

"Sure, but not in here." I now refused to allow anyone to discuss anything related to money or his prognosis in front of him. We walked in silence down the hall to a room filled with tables. This new case manager was older and had salt and pepper hair and thick glasses. I had only met her in person once and had spoken to her over the phone several times. We sat across from each other, and I wondered how I must look to her. It had been just over one year, post injury. I had lost weight and not in the healthy *lose weight* kind of way. I just simply couldn't eat. When I did, it was always at odd hours, or I would just fill my body full of coconut water. I remember once when I was a kid, my dad saying that coconuts were a complete source of nutrition, and that had always stuck with me. I figured if I was ever on a desert island, I would climb trees and eat coconuts. I might as well be on a desert island—that is how I felt most of the time—completely alone and in full survival mode. I drank coconut water every day and sometimes (oftentimes) this was all I would eat or drink. It kept me from getting dehydrated and gave me the energy I needed to keep going. I have no idea what vitamins and minerals coconut water has in it, but now, I am sure that it was not a complete and balanced meal. As time went on, my hair began falling out and my nails began to weaken and break. My skin paled and began to show signs of the stress we lived in. My once full head of curly hair had thinned down to a few wispy curls. My eyes were dark and thickened by lack of sleep. I rarely wore make up these days and generally drew my hair back into a ponytail. I was perpetually cold and often wore a jacket inside the hospital.

I sat across the table from her, my oversized jacket made me feel small. "Well, as I've told you, your insurance stopped paying. Have you figured out what you are going to do?" I cleared my throat.

"No, I mean what do you suggest?" I asked quietly. *She knew our situation. Her question was not one of compassion.*

"Well, we are not getting paid here, and I'm worried it's going to be a huge liability for you. That hospital bill keeps growing every day."

"I realize that, but I don't have any other solutions. I cannot take him home. We have three children. I am going back to work. I don't see how I will be able to care for them and for him safely. Your staff here—they are on for twenty-four hours, and they can barely manage his care. That's with a nurse and doctors around the clock!" She cleared her throat and looked down at her notebook.

"Well, meanwhile, the bill is growing every day. They will come after you. They will take your assets, your home." I sat up straighter in my chair and leaned in as she spoke. She was done playing nice, and I could see a battle starting. She went straight for the jugular. By now, I've learned something about myself—I don't back down from a fight when cornered. Who knew? I always thought of myself as small and weak. My heart pounded in my ears. *God, help me please!* I pleaded in my head. Nothing scared me more than the possibility of losing our home—of the boys having to endure yet another change. She stopped talking and cleared her throat and looked casually at the clock on her phone. "I've gone ahead and called a meeting with our finance and billing department. They can be up here in thirty minutes. I think if you hear it from them, it might motivate you to take some action.

"What do we owe?" Somehow, in my head, I figured we could pay for some of it from our savings and maybe the rest could be made into a payment plan.

"Last time we checked, it was at eight-hundred thousand," she said coolly.

"Eight-hundred thousand?" *How could it be so high?*

She smiled at my disbelief. "He's at a very high cost here and it goes up every day." I laughed. It was a nervous laugh, but a laugh, nonetheless. *Take the house, God—take it! Just take it. It wasn't enough to take my husband, break up our family and now this?* My thoughts were angry thoughts. In my head, I heard him answer me. *Daughter, your husband is STILL here. He will be healed.* My anger stopped in its tracks. Arnoldo *was* still here.

"Well, the hospital has to do what they need to do. I get it. It's a business. I just want to go on record that I am asking you to discharge him."

"To home?"

"NO, he is not safe at home."

"Oh, ok. Well, then we are back where we started." She fumbled with her notebook again.

"Yes, I suppose we are."

"Let's regroup here in thirty minutes." I nodded and walked back to Arnoldo's room. He was sitting peacefully in his chair. Tears rolled down my cheeks. Tears of anger, of anguish, frustration. When would this all end? I didn't want to cry in front of him, but I also did not want anyone from his unit to see my tears. Muffled sobs escaped my throat. I heard Arnoldo shift in his chair and cough. He was worried. I mopped my face with a towel.

"It's ok, babe. I'm ok—just frustrated and mad. That lady is awful—but I GOT this—don't worry." I glanced at the clock in his room. I only had a few more minutes before the finance office was to meet me. I straightened my hair, dabbed the underside of my eyes, and cleared my throat. I motioned to his nurse that I was going into a meeting.

"We got him, don't worry. We always keep a good eye on Noni," he smiled. I walked down the hall and felt my heart pounding. I felt like a warrior walking into battle alone. But I wasn't alone---*God, help me!* I cried out. I straightened my jacket and stood tall. I was ready to battle. When I entered the room, I saw that the case manager and all three women from the finance office were already seated at a round table. They each stood up and introduced themselves. One was a supervisor and the others her staff. The case manager led the meeting and started out by saying that insurance had stopped paying weeks ago.

"I just want her to know that the bill is growing and that eventually the hospital will need to collect."

One of the ladies turned to me and asked, "Gabby, have you applied for government assistance?" I had inquired and had gotten the paperwork started but wasn't hopeful. We had already been denied once before. I had hired a lawyer. I shared that information with the group. "Second, tell me about you. You have kids? How is your husband doing?" Her eyes looked soft and kind. God had stepped in. He had never left.

171

The rest of the meeting revolved around our family. We spoke about what had happened to Arnoldo—how the kids were in the car, how he was saved and alive, and how we had all been unharmed on that freeway. We spoke about how he had gone home and was now back in the hospital. I shared with them about his debilitating spasms and the renewed storming and all of the unknowns. One of the ladies wiped her eyes, while the other looked uncomfortable as she handed me a letter.

"I'm supposed to give this to you, but I'm praying that you get the government benefits." Inside, the letter showed a bill for $1.2 million. "It is about twenty thousand dollars per day for him here, so it changes daily." I nodded and folded the letter. We stood and each one of them hugged me.

"Would you like to meet him?" They looked at each other. "Come on, come meet the man we are speaking about—he's just down the hall." I had already started walking, they couldn't say no. They walked with me, as did the case manager. She had been silent for most of the meeting. As we stepped into his room, I saw that Arnoldo was back in his bed. "Here he is." I introduced each one, and they politely introduced themselves. "He understands everything you are saying. His body just hasn't fully connected, so his movements are difficult." I stopped talking as they walked around his room looking at the smiling photographs of our family taken just months before.

"Your boys are so young," commented one of the ladies. "So, so young." We spoke for a while longer, and I assured them that Arnoldo was making strides to get better.

"Arnoldo, raise your arm if you have full faith that you are going to walk out of here." I asked him. He raised his arm.

"Oh!" They all exclaimed. People are often surprised when he responds despite all my assurances that he can hear and process well. They all hugged me and wished us well as they left. "Don't worry—you just keep focusing on getting better and you—" she turned to me, "you have to be strong for your husband and kids. It will all work out. We are praying for you. St. Jude, he is the patron saint of impossible cases. Get his candle. Pray for intercession." I nodded, feeling so, so loved. More hugs and well wishes and they were gone.

I sat down at the edge of Arnoldo's bed and reflected on the day. God had stepped in, took over and guided the meeting, and assured me that all would be well. My heart soared with his love. *Nothing is impossible with God.*

Dear Sweetie,

It's just a pick-up truck— a 2015 black GMC Sierra half-ton. Nothing but metal and plastic molded together. Yet, as I hand over the keys to the man at the consignment shop, my heart is heavy. It's just a truck, but in a way, it is a piece of you. Part of me is happy to get this over with—this truck—this truck was where our lives changed. Your cardiac arrest happened in this truck. This is where we were all together as a family, before your illness. This truck has memories—beautiful ones— like you saving up for it, looking for it, being excited to finally buy something for yourself. It's just a material possession—it doesn't matter, and it shouldn't matter. Yet, it still hurts. Our last road trip together, before the accident, was in this truck. As we pulled into the quaint, Gold Rush town of Nevada City, snow flurries floated around us. I felt exhilarated at the snow and opened the window, relishing the crisp, cold air. You reached across the center console and grabbed my hand. "You are so beautiful," you whispered. "I love our life...it's so amazing—it's almost too good to be true." How I wish you had never said that. How I wish I could go back in time to that moment and relive the love, gratitude, peace, and JOY that I felt in that moment. The snow, JUST US, our love, looking for adventure together. One thing is for sure—we are always up for adventure. That remains true to this day.

I love you so much, Arnoldo. God is asking me to write to bring people to him—I feel it—I know this in my heart, and I have to say that we must ask God to help us—to allow us time, to give me peace and help

with all my earthly tasks. I know you want to obey, and I want to obey—
we will answer the call, but we need guidance and help from God. I pray
that he helps us.

Gabby

PRINCESS OZMA

If all the beasts were gone, men would die from a great loneliness of spirit, for whatever happens to the beasts also happens to the man. All things are connected. Whatever befalls the Earth befalls the sons of the Earth.

Chief Seattle

Wednesday, September 19, 2018

Dearest Arnoldo,

A chapter in our lives closed today. My heart is broken. Our beloved cat, our sweet and loving Princess Ozma, left this world in my arms today. I was alone and I can't tell you how much that hurt. She was 18 years old. Beautiful and loving and strong until the end. Just a cat, I'm sure many will say, but in my soul, and I know in your soul, she was much more than that. Our Ozzies was the first living thing we had to care for as a "couple." We found her at the Humane Society together and she chose us to be her human parents. I remember going there to look at dogs. I didn't want a cat. You didn't want any pets. So funny, that the moment we walked into the cat area, we both began playing with the kittens. As we were ready to leave, a little black paw hit my shoulder, and I saw this tiny black kitten with huge ears and beautiful emerald-green eyes looking at me with a look of pure longing and love.

When I held her in my arms, she curled up and fell asleep, and I knew she was ours. I sat on our back porch the other day with tears streaming down my cheeks, reflecting on her life and why there was so much pain in my heart. In large part, it was because of who she was, but an even bigger part of it was what she represented. Ozma had been there from the beginning. She was part of us before we got married—she knew us as we grew in our relationship and eventually married. She was there when we bought our first home together and got to relish and enjoy the excitement we all felt together. When Ozma discovered the outdoors, I rejoiced with her as she discovered ants and bugs moving on the ground.

Remember when I wanted to walk her like you would a dog with a leash and a collar and she laid flat on the ground and refused to move? I'll never forget you laughing at me and reminding me that she wasn't a dog. Yet, we trained her to fetch and to sit and shake and roll over on command. She did it willingly when she wanted to, but as you would expect with any cat, ignored us and gave us a look of absolute disdain at will. Every morning, she happily purred and talked to us with helicopter sounds as we poured her food into her bowl. We taught her to love the water and baths. She loved you most though. She loved curling up next to you as you sat reading your books and drinking your coffee each morning. She brought us love and peace and such entertainment. Remember how high she would jump to get the ball as we played catch? Remember how she would flatten out her body as we squeezed her under the couch to get the ball? And my personal favorite was how she would squeeze herself into my purse every day, in the hopes that I would take her to work with me.

Ozma was there for you through your job promotions, for every account you broke, for every deal you made. She was there when I started law school. During the stress of my final exams she purred contently at my feet while I studied. She reminded me to take breaks, to eat, to look up from my books for a second and love her. She was our mediator during arguments and reminded us to be respectful and kind to each other. Ozma was there at home waiting during the birth of each of our children. She welcomed her human brothers with such grace and loving patience. She was there as they discovered her and allowed them to pet her and even managed to make it through their toddler years as they squeezed her a little too tight or pulled her tail. I always imagined Princess Ozma as a mother herself. Had she had kittens, she would have made an excellent momma. Every child that came across her loved her. We even had a note placed on our door with a drawing made by the little neighborhood children that thanked us for her and for allowing them to love her and pet her. Do you remember?

Ozma was there during our tough economic times and there for us as we rejoiced in God's abundance. Ozma was there when my mother got sick. During the long stressful days of her illness, Ozma found my mother's room and didn't leave her side. That was her way. She always went to the person that needed her the most and offered all of herself to them. She was there for me when my father died, during my multiple miscarriages, and during the ups and downs of marriage and parenting. Ozma was there for me when you got sick. She was my comfort and company at night when I was tired or upset. Ozma worried about you too and got sick herself when you didn't come home. She loves you so much. When our house was in upheaval and disarray, she was our constant reminder of better times, of the joys of the past and the hopes of the future. Ozma rejoiced when you came home. She regained weight that she had lost and for several months began looking like her old self. When you returned to the hospital, she too began losing weight, and I knew that something was wrong. I begged her to wait for you to come home, but her physical body could not hold on to this world anymore. In the last weeks, I gave her permission to go. She left this world knowing how much we both loved her. She knew that she was a huge piece of our past—almost two decades of love and joy, sorrow and difficulties, interwoven with faith and prayer.

When our little Nico was saying goodbye to her on the morning of her last day on earth, he asked me, "Mommy where is she going? She's broken and won't be able to walk." In the end, her hind legs were completely paralyzed, and he was worried about her. I wanted to explain death to him, and I realized that I did not know exactly what to say to a 3-year-old. So, I told him that she was going to a farm where animals were healed and that she would be all better and she would be able to run and jump and chase dogs and lizards. Our gorgeous Princess Ozma would be able to lay in the sun and make friends with other animals that lived on this farm. The farm has a beautiful Victorian farmhouse attached with warm couches and beds and many human friends to love and pet the animals.

"Mommy, I want to go there too," he said immediately.

"One day, my little Nico. We will all go there and see our Ozma again." Nico smiled and accepted my answer. One day, we will all be reunited again. Our little family, our beloved pets, together again. For now, our journey is not complete on this earth, and we will continue to be guided by God until we reach the other side. Oh, Arnoldo, I hope you heal soon and come home. We miss and love you so much. I cannot wait to complete our earthly mission together. God has big plans for us. Have faith.

With Love,

Your Gabby

REFLECTION

*"For I know the plans I have for you, declares the LORD, plans for welfare
and not for evil, to give you a future and a hope."*

Jeremiah 29:11 (ESV)

When things go well in life, we are thankful but don't cry out to God. I have come to the conclusion that this is the time where we need to cry out to God even more, to guide us and to help others. We need to cry out to God for help on how to be his warriors here on earth. When things are going well in our lives, it is easy to forget this. It is easy to bask in the golden sun of complacency, and it is easy to take the time for granted. I have been reflecting on my life before Arnoldo got sick—before my mom got sick—before my dad passed. My reflections are on my easy life, when my biggest stress was wondering what we were having for dinner, or whether Arnoldo would be home from work in time to take the boys to basketball practice. Sure, we had all the general worries parents have—the boys are not eating enough good food, too much junk food, too much screen time, not enough reading, are we putting enough away for retirement, can we afford another trip this year, can we figure out more time to spend together as a married couple?? The list goes on and on. Knowing what I know now—being in the eye of a storm that ripped our family apart, piece by piece, threatening the security of our family—I wish I had been STILL more often. I wish I had seen the time before the storm for what it was supposed to be—a time to grow closer to God; not only to give thanks, but to cry out to him and ask, Lord, guide me—use me for your glory. Lead me in your path.

Every single one of us, every single human being, is given a purpose. It is up to us to learn our purpose and to choose to walk in that purpose. We are all given an opportunity to make an impact on our world, on our fellow brothers and sisters in the world. What we do in our lives is always up to us. The choices are ours. If we all would stop, in the busyness of the world, be STILL, and listen to our call, this world would be a changed world. You see, the call is ever present in every moment of every day. Love can flow in our heart, in our minds—it can be as simple as lifting up a friend, offering words of positivity to strangers, co-workers, loved ones. I actually used to feel that if I wasn't in the trenches in a war-torn country, feeding the homeless, or fundraising for victims of poverty, then it didn't matter. In my opinion, it didn't matter because what I could do was too small. This is a LIE. We may not all have the ability to become Red Cross volunteers, or pull people out of burning buildings, but God has equipped each and every one of us with the tools to do his work here on earth.

Prayer. Pray for other people every day. Pray for your coworker with cancer, your neighbor whose brother just died, the stranger on the street asking for change. We ALL can pray. Be intentional about praying and do it often. Praying is simply a conversation with God and asking him in that conversation to be present in the lives of others. Yes, it's that simple.

Deny negativity. Only allow thoughts of love to enter your mind and exit your mouth or fingertips. I mention fingertips because in the age of social media, we need to be more aware than ever. The phrase, the pen is mightier than the sword, comes to mind—or it should read, the keyboard is mightier than the sword. What we write to and about others has an impact. It has an impact not just on that individual, but on the world around us. It impacts every single person that reads that comment because it forms an emotion and feeling in that person. A few years ago, a young boy in our community made a mistake and committed a crime. He was criticized and ostracized on social media for months, ultimately resulting in the boy taking his own life. Stories like these are much too familiar and commonplace, and there should be no room in the world for them. Hurting others from the comfort of our homes—behind the walls of cyberspace—is much too easy. Here is where we must stop and allow God to come in. Give every word and thought to God—before replying, before reacting, before typing!

Arnoldo would often come home from work angry, hurt, and frustrated by the actions of a particular coworker. This coworker would make belittling comments to him or make poor decisions and was unkind to him and others around her. One particular day, Arnoldo was very upset because this coworker had made an error and had caused a huge issue in an account. He had called her, and true to form, she denied her actions and refused to remedy the situation. He had kept his composure at work but came home angry and frustrated.

"She won't fix the error, let alone admit that it was her actions that caused it," he had ranted. I was proud at him for not getting angry at her and for first seeking a way to work through his frustrations. I asked him if he wanted to pray. He agreed and we prayed for her heart, her mind, and for the situation. We asked God to take over. The next day, he called me excitedly from work. She had called him to apologize for causing the issue and offered to work with him on how to fix it! God answered our prayers. This example seems trite in light of the storm we are passing through now, but I am writing about it to illustrate that no matter what our earthly problems are—God cares. He wants to be involved. He wants to help us. Nothing is too small or too big. Nothing is impossible with God. Nothing is possible without God.

When we are going through seasons of peace and joy—take the strength of those moments to help those around you. While we must be a warrior for God at all times, when we are going through storms, we are so busy hanging on while the winds are blowing that it is much more difficult to help others. It is not impossible—but definitely more difficult. So, take those moments of peace and pray and work actively, with all your ability, to lift others up who need you. In reflection, I wish I had been more of a warrior for God during our time of peace. However, I look forward to doing this in the future. Peace will come for us, and using what I know now, I know that I can do more for this world.

SPIRITUAL WARFARE

"For our struggle is not against flesh and blood, but against the rulers, against the authorities, against the powers of this dark world and against the spiritual forces of evil in the heavenly realms."

Ephesians 6:12 (NIV)

I was very reluctant to write about spiritual warfare in this book. In my head I reasoned that I did not want to give the darkness any of my time or acknowledgement. However, God urged me to write about it. He revealed to me that by exposing darkness through light—the darkness ceases to exist. My hope in this chapter is to bring light to the dark, and in turn, help others recognize it and defeat it. Like it or not, if you are reading this, you are a warrior of God. God is calling upon you now, more than ever, to fight the dark. Yet, you must know the battle plan and have the armor to do so. I am by no means an expert. I am learning as I go. But I will share with you my experiences and hope that you can use them in your own lives to help you.

For a large part of my childhood and early adulthood, I believed that Satan did not exist. How could he exist, I reasoned, if God made the world and God is love? Why would there be this dark force? It didn't make sense in my mind. To believe in him was to give power to him, and I simply could not. One key difference between who I was then and who I am now is the fact that I was not suffering at that point in my life as I am now. I had a fairly normal childhood, filled with loving parents, loving family, and friends. Of course, there were the small growing pains of losing good friends when we moved to another city in my teen years, the heartbreak of first love, and the insecurities of adolescence—but I was in a warm loving household and did not suffer as I know many children have and do. I say this because I do believe that external forces affect our view of the world. I was raised as a Christian by two devout Catholic parents that encouraged us to read and question while gaining knowledge. I have fond memories of being in bed as a child and being awakened by the sounds of a chair scraping the floor in the kitchen, the cupboards opening and closing, the stove being turned on . . . These were the sounds of my father who was up before 5 am every morning to read the Bible. I still remember the sound of him drinking his coffee as he turned the pages in his Bible, the way he cleared his throat as he read, and how he sometimes read passages out loud that he loved or needed to reflect upon. How I wish I would have discussed this topic with my father before he passed away.

As I grew into adulthood, I began to understand that I was wrong about Satan. Not only is he very much real, he thrives on people, like me, not believing he exists. If he doesn't exist, then nobody will try to defeat him. It is as if he is wearing an invisible cloak, and he can come and go as he pleases. His one and only plan is to destroy all of God's creations. That includes you and me, my children, your children and grandchildren. By destruction, I don't just mean physical destruction, I mean the destruction of our very souls. We are made in God's image, and God is LOVE. Therefore, we are love. Satan is the opposite. He is the darkness, the fear, the anxiety, the anger, the hate. In war, having an invisible cloak would be a powerful weapon for the enemy, as he could come and go as he pleases—undetected. Satan operates in much the same way when people deny his existence. He has the freedom to come and go as he pleases.

Again, I want to confess right now to you that I was reluctant to write about this. Even though I was raised in a strong Christian household, the devil was rarely mentioned. The churches we attended rarely mentioned him during the homilies. In fact, I cannot remember even one sermon that addressed the topic directly. There was a lot alluding to him and hinting at his evil works, but there was never a clear definition of who he is and the destruction he can cause. So, it was much easier for me to not think about him or talk about it. Later in my life, I began to see his affect on the world through the dark and evil acts of people. It was as though a veil had been lifted from my eyes.

Despite finally understanding this, my life was full of distractions, and as I have come to understand, these very distractions are the mitochondria that power the cells of evil. I will talk about this in more detail a bit later. First, I want to talk about materialism. In a previous chapter, I have already mentioned materialism, and I mention it again because, in this country and in our world, this is a HUGE one. The pursuit of material possessions has become the new idolatrous religion. I want to be clear here that this can affect all of us—rich and poor alike. It can be as simple as the desire to work more hours to buy your child those special basketball shoes, or the desire for more real estate to add to your retirement portfolio. Am I saying that we should not want abundance in our lives? NO. What I am saying is that it should not become the center of our lives. God is our center and anything that replaces him comes from darkness. It is good to live in abundance. God wants us to be cared for and joyous, but he does NOT want us to leave him.

Another powerful weapon used by Satan is *distraction*. Distractions come in the form of innocent TV shows, social media, cell phones, sports for your child, extra-curricular activities, work, and the list goes on. I want to first mention these because, on the outside, they are seemingly benign and harmless. However, they have become the center of so many families in today's modern world. If you are *too busy* driving your child back and forth from activity to activity, working long hours, on social media, on phones, watching tv, etc.—then stop and be STILL. These *too busy* hours are time away from God. There is nothing Satan loves more than to pull a family away from God.

Our family, before Arnoldo's illness, was very distracted. We lived the suburban modern *busy* life of school, work, sports, music, dance, etc. I know that, in my head, I justified all of this by thinking, *we are doing all of this for our children, how can any of this be bad?* By itself, it is not bad, but it distracted the boys and us from our real purpose. Arnoldo and I wanted to raise these little men to be warriors in Christ, but nothing we did was preparing them. We did not show them how to put Christ first. Instead, we showed them how to put themselves first. This had the opposite effect of what we wanted for them. So how do we reconcile the desire to give our children experiences and enrichment and also raise them to be warriors of God? Make everything about God. Put God first in all we do. If they are having trouble in a subject, pray with them about it. If they do not like their teachers, help them pray for those teachers. If they are being driven to piano and music and dance and baseball and basketball, take those moments to pray with them. If it is too much, and it is taking away from God, then let things go. Always put God first. Always put God first. Show them through *your* actions that God comes first. I know, firsthand, that this is not easy to do. I know that I am making mistakes every day and am not always sure whether what I am doing is right. If this is you, pray about it. Ask for help. He is *always* with you. He is waiting to help. Allow God to be your center, so that anything you do comes from him.

There is also the not-so-hidden spiritual warfare that affects our daily life and world. I mentioned materialism and distraction as Satan's game plan for the modern world. Yet, there is more, much more. With the pain of seeing Arnoldo go through so much over the past year, our household and life felt chaotic. I became overwhelmed and that feeling of overwhelming stress brought me to a point of anger that I had never felt before. I lost my temper at the children and the world around me. In addition, things at home began breaking left and right. In a matter of months, our upstairs air conditioner began leaking water and leaked through the ceiling in the hallway. Then, several months later, the motor on the unit broke. Our garage refrigerator leaked and broke. The inside of the shower (a pipe) in my master bedroom leaked through the floor and ceiling into the kitchen below. Then, a pipe outside connected to our sprinkler system broke and water gushed for two days, without my knowledge, causing a huge bill. Water from the rain eroded the siding on our house and began to leak and destroy the structure of the house. The outside pergola over our deck became eroded and destroyed with the water. I shared my frustrations with one of my neighbors and he chalked all of these issues up to coincidence—how could it be anything else? The homes were older, and things break. What puzzled me is the frequency and the fact that they happened within a short time of each other. All of them happened within months of each other.

Things in the house would suddenly go missing—remotes for the television, keys, etc.—and then be found later, with no explanation as to how they got there. This only added to the chaos. I will never forget one particular instance when my oldest son could not find the lanyard and keys he wore around his neck every day. We live in a gated community, and there is a small gate across the street from the elementary school that can only be accessed with a key. My son was old enough to ride his scooter to and from home and wore the key around his neck to get himself in and out of the gate. One morning, the key was not where it was supposed to be. He was late for school and I was angry. "Mom, I hung up the key. I know I did," he pointed to the place on the wall.

"If you hung up the key, it would be there." I was frustrated. We took apart the key rack and searched high and low, and the lanyard and keys were nowhere to be found. We searched his backpack, the car, the coatrack, thinking it might have fallen. *Nothing.* We gave up. I gave him my gate key and made a mental note to make additional copies of the gate keys in order to have extra. Two weeks later, we woke up and found the lanyard hanging on the key rack. I thought that maybe he or someone else in the house had found the key, but no one knew how they had gotten there. My son looked just as surprised as I was.

In addition, during this time, my two-year old son would wake up terrified and point to areas of his room where he explained that he saw *monsters*. The two-year-old imagination is very vivid, and I explained this all away as normal behavior for his age. One day, during nap time, he told me that he saw a "mommy" on his wall. "Mommy" was his way of describing a woman. He pointed at something and said, "See, there she is." The more I asked about her, the more I realized that he was seeing something that was unseen by my eyes. He told me that the mommy's name was Burney and that the mommy would ask him questions about his brothers. *What was this? Was this an angel?* I had read stories about children being able to see guardian angels. However, my son was terrified and that was enough for me to know that this could not be from God. He did not feel comfortable being in his room alone whenever he saw this apparition. One day, prior to his nap, he pointed to a spot on the wall and asked me why she was there. He looked terrified. I had had enough. I lifted him out of his crib and brought him downstairs. I took holy water and walked into his room, proclaiming Jesus as our Lord and Savior, commanding whatever was there to leave, in Jesus' name, if it was not from God. I prayed over each part of his room and commanded anything not of God to leave and never to return, in Jesus' name. I proclaimed that this was God's house, over and over. When I was finished, I realized that I was yelling because Nico was calling for me and asked me if *Burney* had tried to hurt me. "No, baby, she cannot hurt me, and she cannot hurt you because you have Jesus in your heart." When he walked back into his room, he looked around and proclaimed, "Mommy, she is gone!" He stopped seeing anything in his room after this day.

I began praying for God's help and it came immediately. Within weeks, a friend who had been inviting me to her church for months, invited me again and this time I accepted. The sermon had to do with understanding and acknowledging that we all had Jesus inside of us but that there were evil forces trying to thwart God's plan. The message was "what is in us is stronger than what is *on* us." A confirmation that there were forces at work attempting to hurt us, but that God was always with us. I felt a renewed strength.

Later, I posted on social media that I was looking for a bible study group to join. What I needed was a mentor, but I did not know it at the time. I needed someone that could help me wade through these unfamiliar waters. I was contacted by a distant cousin that I had never met. She offered her help and our spiritual mentoring began. She was the answer to my prayers. God had sent me a personal guide to show me exactly what to do. She helped me wade through the fear and chaos I was experiencing and always directed me to scripture. I shared with her what was happening in our home. "These are spiritual attacks," she affirmed. "Your family is being attacked." This seemed surreal to me—like a movie. What was this? Things like this didn't happen outside of Hollywood, did they? Yet, they were happening. There wasn't a logical explanation for any of it. She warned me that there could be more to come.

"What? Why?" I asked.

"Because, your entire family has grown so close to God, and there is work that you will all do to help others—HIS work. Satan does not want that."

This was the beginning of a new war for me. I finally began to see what I was battling and how to defeat it. This same family member led me to look in the Bible for help. Specifically, she led me to Ephesians 6:11-18. *[11] Put on the whole armor of God, that you may be able to stand against the schemes of the devil. [12] For we do not wrestle against flesh and blood, but against the rulers, against the authorities, against the cosmic powers over this present darkness, against the spiritual forces of evil in the heavenly places. [13] Therefore take up the whole armor of God, that you may be able to withstand in the evil day, and having done all, to stand firm. [14] Stand therefore, having fastened on the belt of truth, and having put on the breastplate of righteousness, [15] and, as shoes for your feet, having put on the readiness given by the gospel of peace. [16] In all circumstances take up the shield of faith, with which you can extinguish all the flaming darts of the evil one; [17] and take the helmet of salvation, and the sword of the Spirit, which is the word of God, [18] praying at all times in the Spirit, with all prayer and supplication. To that end, keep alert with all perseverance, making supplication for all the saints.*

As we read through the scripture, I felt a strength come over me that could only come from the word of God. This battle was not new—Satan and all his demons had always existed. Their agenda to destroy humans was not new. God had specifically given his people armor and protection to fight. One week after reading this, a friend invited me to a women's devotion. I knew no one and hesitated, but an unseen force led me to go. The group leader spoke to the handful of women in attendance and said, "I had another scripture to read for us today, but God led me to Ephesians 6:11-18, the Armor of God. I feel as though this is what we need to read and pray on today." I felt chills running through my body. God was showing me and affirming what I needed.

After this meeting, I had a revelation that we all need the Armor of God. It is something to read, contemplate, pray on, and start each and every day with. We are all being attacked every single day. The attacks come as negative feelings, thoughts, actions, fear, anxiety, and sin. Satan wants an opening—an edge on you and your loved ones. We have the tools to stop him. YES, we do. All the hate you see in the world, on the news, on the road, in social media—yes, it can all be halted. Put on your Armor of God every day and fight.

I could write an entire book on the *Armor of God* because this scripture outlines, in great detail, a battle plan for all of us to follow. I will do my best to condense everything to a few paragraphs. First, God is showing us and confirming that the devil does exist. He affirms that there are evil spirits and that our battle is not with the physical. Second, he instructs us to put on the *whole* Armor of God in order to resist Satan. He starts with the belt of *truth*. What is God talking about here? It is the truth about who you are. The truth that you are a child of God. That you are made in his image and that you are *Love,* just as he is *Love.* God is and will always be a part of you. God *LOVES* you and knowing that is VERY important in this battle plan because Satan loves to whisper lies that we are not worthy, that we are not good enough. . . .. The truth is that we have inherited the kingdom of heaven as believers in Jesus Christ. Jesus came to show us the *way, the truth, and the life.* So, don't believe anything else. Know who you are. Remind yourself every morning that you are a daughter or son of the Most High. *Believe.*

Second, is *righteousness*. This is your breastplate. As armor goes, the breastplate protects the most surface area of the body. Here, God is asking us to remember *righteousness.* To know that this *truth* that he has revealed to us is the moral and right way. He is asking you *not* to waver. Not to back down when someone comes in with a different view or is ready to tear you down. Stand firm in who you are and what you know and live a life that is pleasing to God by following in the path he has set before you. Practically, this means to put God at the center of your life. It means to question what you hear, what you read, what you watch, and ask whether it is in line with what God is asking of you. *Hold every thought captive.* Present it to God before letting it inside your heart.

Third is having shoes of *readiness* on our feet. In other words, be ready. Do not be caught off-guard. Do not allow distractions and other things to come and try to lure you away. Be ready and willing to hear God speak to you and obey.

Fourth, hold up your shield of *faith . . . in all circumstances.* Life is fragile, it is ever-changing, it is messy and ugly and unfair, and not the picture-perfect world we all want or expect. Faith is what we all need to have in ALL our circumstances. Hold up that shield of faith during the calm, peaceful days, and hold it up strong during the storms. Faith is what will get you through. It will also be what will help others. Your *faith,* your willingness to hold that shield for others, will be what will help them. I cannot tell you how many times my faith would waver. Countless times. There were times on my way to and from the hospital, when I would imagine my car moving, ever so slightly to the right, and hitting the barrier and going over the cliff and just ending this life. Yes, I would think this dreadful thought because my pain was too much . . . it was overwhelming, it was dark and ugly, and more than what I thought I could handle. Yet, it was the faith of others that held me together. The countless number of people standing in the gap for me. Those people included strangers, people that I had just met, and friends and family. It is funny how some of the people that I most imagined to be here for us during difficult times are the people that were not here at all—and the people that I never imagined to be here, were here every step of the way with us. If your life is in a season of peace and abundance, be the shield of faith for others. Help them stand up, steady them, and hold their shield for them until they can hold it themselves. There are angels that saved my life. God only knows how he used them to say the right thing at the right time to help keep me going. Listen to the voice of God and obey if he is asking you to pray for others. My boys are such angels. Their faith has been unwavering. I hate that they have been there for me more than I have been there for them. As a mom, it is hard to acknowledge that, but it is true. They have held me up by their simple statements of absolute and wholehearted faith. So, pray about your faith. Remember to pray a prayer of power over you and your loved ones and your situation.

Fifth, remember to wear the *helmet of salvation.* Yes, this is just a temporary life. We are but pilgrims on our way to our eternal life. We don't understand this. We are distracted and busy with other things . . . but we are saved through Jesus Christ. Remember this and wear that helmet each and every day. Visualize yourself putting on each piece of God's armor. Think about what wearing that helmet means for you.

Sixth, hold the *sword of the spirit, which is the Word of God.* The *Word.* Read the Bible. Start with the gospels. Read, read, and read some more. Join a bible study group. Start your own. Find a person to have tea or coffee with and read together. Read it out loud as a family. Buy Bibles for your children and start with simple stories. The Word of God is the sword! Think about a battle. We have the armor to protect us, but where is our weapon? The Word of God is the sword . . . the weapon that will destroy the darkness. Why? Because within it is the *truth.* I can assure you that I am not an expert in biblical studies. I have read different parts of the Bible but have not read it cover to cover. There are parts of the Bible that I do not understand or know. However, each and every time I pray and open up the Bible, something new is revealed to me. Something that God wants me to know. We are human, and we forget, or we don't have time. Make time. This is our greatest weapon against the dark forces. If you feel anxious, or fearful, or worried . . . open up the Bible and meditate on the passage that God reveals to you. He wants to talk to you. He wants to help you. Allow him in and allow him to speak to you. I believe that God speaks to us in many ways. Sometimes it is through other people, or books, or music, or artwork . . . Be open and willing to hear him. Fill your every thought with God.

Finally, *prayer.* This is the last ingredient in the Armor of God, but definitely not the least. Earlier, I wrote about an email that Arnoldo had sent to me in which he highlighted a quote that read, "Faith is the doorway that all miracles come through, but prayer is the key that unlocks the door." I agree with this so much! Prayer is the key to unlock the door. Pray about everything. In the morning, wake up in prayer. What is prayer? A pastor that I highly respect recently spoke to his congregation about prayer. What really stuck with me was that he stressed that prayer is simply a conversation with God! It is not a job interview, where you have to be at your best and have your notecards with you or memorize your speech. It is just a conversation with someone who not only intimately knows you—but *loves* you. Here's the amazing part. A conversation is two ways! Therefore, when you are in prayer, be open to hearing God's responses to your prayers.

He will let you know what he wants for you in your life. During this dark storm, God has told me many different things in many different ways, but each time, there was no doubt in my mind that it was God talking to me. Oftentimes, his responses were not what I wanted them to be. I have had many arguments with God when I would hear him wanting to tell me something, but I would want something else. Yes, this was prayer—it was me conversing with God. I remember one time when I was feeling so much pain. The immensity of our situation was holding me captive, and I started to drown in guilt and sorrow. I felt as though I was hanging by a thread. I could not hold on any longer. Negative thoughts filled my head. *It was my fault that Arnoldo was not healed. I didn't have enough faith. It was my fault he was sick. I could have prevented this. I should have done things differently. I didn't fight hard enough. I didn't pray enough...* The list went on and on. Then, I heard God speak, and what he said was so clear and profound that I was absolutely sure it was him. He said: *"How can you believe that? To believe that is to believe that you have greater power than I. NO—none of this is YOUR fault. It just is—but I am using this tragedy to bring so many people to me. Arnoldo will be healed. Fully. 100%. Not because of something YOU did or did not do, but because of me. I am your Lord God, I am your Father. I am yours and you are mine. I know exactly what is on your heart before you know it. I know this is hard. Don't despair as this is almost over. Believe. Trust. Let all your worries go and place your trust in me. Have I not worked everything out?"*

Talk with him. Tell him your desires and hopes and dreams. Ask him to guide you. Allow him to show you his plan. The miracle is just waiting for you. You just need to turn the key!

During this same conversation, God revealed another profound truth. It was about love. LOVE—a simple word that has become the catalyst for so much in the world, either through it or through its lacking. God is love. We are made in the image of God and therefore, we *are* love. It is who we are and who we are meant to be, regardless of any and all existing external forces. Our souls are pure love and that can never be

194

changed. Christ calls upon us to be his *love in action* through every thought, every word, every action. Arnoldo and I have seen this love come through during the worst part of our storm, and there is love coming through yet. People have brought meals, given money, clothes, toys, surprises at our doorstep, and offered help. *Love in action.* Our neighbors have taken our trash in and out since Arnoldo has been in the hospital for the better part of a year. *Love in action.* Other neighbors built a wheelchair ramp for Arnoldo. Other friends have helped with the animals while we are not home. His family, particularly his youngest sister, has lovingly cared for Arnoldo every day that I am not in the hospital with him. She has also taken care of our boys to allow me to be there with him. This is all *love in action.*

God revealed to me something new about the Prayer of Power revelation he had given Arnoldo. In my own understanding, a Prayer of Power was *faith.* It was having the faith like a mustard seed and praying a prayer so full of faith that it could move mountains. Yet, God revealed to me that there is a very key ingredient that is needed in order for us to pray and truly have faith. This key ingredient is *love.* Fill yourself and those around you with God's love before, during, and after prayer. Fill them and you with love for Jesus Christ, who loves all of us. That politician you do not agree with, the thief that took your purse, that girl that called you names, the doctor that was dismissive, the case manager that was unkind, the man that cut you off—every single one is loved by God. Fill your hearts with love, so you can love as Christ loves—so you can show grace, as Christ shows us grace, so we can speak for them and for their salvation. Jesus Christ wants all of us in his kingdom, not *some* of us. He wants *you.* LOVE. *For God so loved the world that he gave his one and only Son, that whoever believes in him shall not perish but have eternal life. John 3:16.* God sacrificed his son for us. For Love.

Love is key because the entire reason for Faith, the entire point of all of our existence is to love and be loved—even when it is difficult and seemingly impossible to do so. *What about when people do evil things? What about when someone is filled with such hate that they commit atrocities?* Love. Yes, even then—love. Love them because God loves them. Jesus Christ has asked us to walk in his path, and Jesus would not want us to live with hate and anger in our hearts. To forgive is to love. To truly forgive is to love them as Christ loves and to love yourself the way he loves you. Be strong in love. It has the power to conquer ALL. Don't you see, you can believe in salvation, have faith, have righteousness, have truth, etc... but all of these are the branches of the love God has for YOU. To truly believe, to have faith, to know the Word of God, we must know that he loves us and calls on us to love. We must teach our children this truth. They must be filled with love. The Prayer of Power must be rooted in love above all else. Love fills us. Love.

November 2, 2018

Dear Arnoldo,

Hey, sweetie, I met with the doctors today—both of your doctors and your case manager. We sat in an office that was probably meant to be a linen closet—it was small and narrow and smelled of lemon polish. Your future. Your prognosis. You. That was the discussion. I was alone with them—just *me* and them.

"It's been close to a year since he was admitted. There has been no consistency in his status. It's not likely that you will see him improve much beyond what we see now." As they talked, my thoughts wandered. My eyes focused on the black shiny leather of the male doctor's shoes. I remembered when you would wear your dress shoes—every single day— to the office. Beautiful Italian leather—walking into meetings and conquering the world. Suddenly, a sense of knowing and understanding came over me. *Document this day and these words because when Arnoldo makes a full and complete recovery, this day will forever be in all our memories and all will be astonished and come to the Lord.* That is what I felt and understood in this moment.

"He will need a lower level of care and will still require twenty-four-hour assistance—it is now custodial care. He will have his G-tube long-term. We do not expect that he will ever be able to have this removed. His dystonia is typical for someone with a brain injury as severe as his. The rigidity and stiffness are to be expected. He's lucky it is not worse. Most patients look like pretzels with this type of injury. You can expect this to get worse. We've never seen someone with an anoxic injury get better from this—not in the cases we've seen here in the hospital."

I did not have it in me to fight or argue. I listened. I asked the Holy Spirit to come over all of us in the room. I did it silently, in my head. I felt at peace as they spoke—peace surrounded me. I heard God speak. *"Those words are not true—those are limitations that they have."*

My love, if God had not held my hand during that meeting—I don't know what I would have done. These are the *HOPE* doctors. They focus on rehabilitation and bring with them hope and healing. Yet, here they were with the grimmest possible news.

"I know we saw a remarkable improvement last year, in August, but it is likely that he will never even reach that level again."

This day—the day of the meeting—your muscle spasms were severe. Maybe you sensed the energy in the room, or maybe you felt the heaviness in my heart—the uncertainty. God held my hand—but I waivered, if for just a moment. SO, here's the thing—despite the grim news, I feel as though your healing and homecoming are near! So near, in fact, that I felt that nervous and giddy feeling, like when you are expecting company and you have to get your house ready! I want you to know that this letter . . . this meeting . . . I have decided not to read aloud to you. It really isn't for you. I felt that this letter is for the world—when you are healed and home and doing what was thought to be impossible—we will always have this letter as a reminder of God's promise and our faith in that promise. One day, you will read this letter and know what was said about you and know that God did not allow human understanding to come in the way of his work. I love you.

November 4, 2018

Dear Sweetie,

I haven't slept on my side of the bed for eighteen months. Since that first night alone, I could not bring myself to do it—to look over at your side, now empty and cold, was too much. I decided to sleep where you slept—so that I never had to look at your empty side of the bed. Today, I felt as though it was time for me to make room for you. That today, it was time for me to sleep on my side, so that I could make room for your homecoming! Just the other day, as I was in prayer—I heard God tell me, *"Dearest Daughter, Increase your faith. Believe. He is coming home completely healed. Do not despair or worry about the details—just be obedient in the path I ask you to take. You will hear my direction more clearly, more often. Be ready. Buy him jeans and shirts that fit and new tennis shoes."* Then I heard the number '32', but I don't know what it means. Can you believe this? These are the words I heard!

December 23, 2018

Dear God,

Over a month ago you told me to buy new clothes and shoes for Arnoldo. That same night you showed me the number 32 and I did not understand what it meant. I searched the Psalms, the rest of scripture, and even Googled the number. It wasn't until I was standing in the men's aisle at Target, buying clothes for Arnoldo, that I felt with absolute certainty that his jeans size was 32. Arnoldo has not worn jeans since the day of his cardiac arrest. His wardrobe has been hospital robes, shorts, or active wear. We decided to take family photos this year. Yes, even though

I was reluctant…even though I didn't want to do it…even though he is still in the hospital, I heard you encourage me to do it. I didn't want him in a robe or active wear. So, I decided to buy him new clothes, and it occurred to me that he had lost so much weight that I had absolutely no idea what his pant size was. You whispered *"32"* to me, as I stood in front of the shelf of jeans in the store. I was so sure it was you whispering that I didn't bother to buy any other sizes. They were a perfect fit. He wore a new sweater, new jeans, and his own brown loafers. God, you know those loafers well. Those loafers sit in our closet, day after day, and haunt me with their presence. They were on his feet the day of his accident. One of them ended up on the freeway and the other remained with him as they pulled him into the ambulance. Later that week, when I was given his bag of belongings, I found his torn jeans, wallet, and one brown loafer inside the bag. I thought the other was lost and I went to throw it away but stopped myself for some reason. Later, I discovered the second shoe in the back seat of the truck. One of the rescue crew must have tossed it inside. I placed them in our closet, and they remained there for over a year. Every day, they tease me and remind me of that horrible moment. So today, I decided to change their path. Arnoldo wore them for our family photos. They are now not reminders of fear, but they are part of his journey of faith and recovery and the miracles that have transpired.

M & M'S
(MORE MIRACLES)

*"He performs wonders that cannot be fathomes,
miracles that cannot be counted."*

Job 5:9 (NIV)

There have been countless examples of miraculous occurrences that have surrounded our family throughout this tragedy. I have written about a few but want to write them all down. I want to share them because these are all the ways that God has shown us that he is with us and continues to be with us. The first miracle is the fact that during Arnoldo's cardiac arrest, Arnoldo's truck stopped on the freeway and did not crash and kill us all. How the truck was stopped, I do not know. I do not have a logical explanation. Later, as I was telling a friend of mine about what happened, she went outside to see if there were any signs of damage on the outside of the truck, or to see if perhaps the truck had hit the guardrail. There were none. The truck was still on, and Arnoldo's foot was on the gas when we pulled him out.

Another miracle was the fact that I was not hit by an oncoming car, and the woman that stopped knew CPR and started compressions on him right away, along with the military doctor that stood by her side. Who were these angels? How I wish I could thank them now. What about the man that had flares in his car and placed them all along and around us? Coincidence? Luck? I know it was God. I wrote earlier about Mother Mary speaking to me during a time when I was falling asleep during a massage. Her voice and her message were so clear, and I felt such peace during that moment that I have no doubt it was her. Here is the other part of that story—months later, I told my cousin Nena that story and she began weeping on the phone. "Oh, Gabby," she sobbed. "We were all in so much shock and pain and hurt at what you were going through that I called out to Mother Mary and pleaded for her to cover you with her mantle and bring you comfort. You are just confirming that she answered my prayer." I was floored. God was with us. He was answering prayers.

A treatment was presented to our family that had the possibility of helping with recovery. The doctor that I was referred to did not make any guarantees but did offer some hope. Arnoldo was in so much pain during this time and had been suffering. I checked with our insurance only to discover that it was not covered. Each treatment would cost nine thousand dollars and the doctor recommended at least three treatments. I don't like writing about money let alone having to think about money, but anyone that has gone through a major illness knows that being sick in this country is extraordinarily expensive. Arnoldo was the only income earner in our house and in seconds, his income was gone. In order to keep his insurance going, I was forced to pay over twenty-four hundred dollars per month. The caregiving expenses were astronomical, not to mention just the costs to run our household. The mortgage needed to be paid and the kids still needed food and clothes and money for that special field trip or the book fairs or events at school. The fundraised money from our friends, family, and community was going quickly, and the savings we had been able to access was slowly being eroded. I knew I needed to return to work but at this time could not imagine leaving the boys to be cared for by strangers while I worked. I was Arnoldo's representative while he was sick. I needed to be at the hospital—by his side. He needed me so much. He couldn't speak for himself. I was both mother and father at home and was needed there too. My heart told me it was too soon to return to work full time. God told me to trust. Every time I thought about money, or felt my stomach drop at the thought of our bank account dwindling, I heard God's word in my heart.

"Therefore, I tell you, do not worry about your life, what you will eat or drink; or about your body, what you will wear. Is not life more than food, and the body more than clothes? 26 Look at the birds of the air; they do not sow or reap or store away in barns, and yet your heavenly Father feeds them. Are you not much more valuable than they? 27 Can any one of you by worrying add a single hour to your life[a]?

28 "And why do you worry about clothes? See how the flowers of the field grow. They do not labor or spin. 29 Yet I tell you that not even Solomon in all his splendor was dressed like one of these. 30 If that is how God clothes the grass of the field, which is here today and tomorrow is thrown into the fire, will he not much more clothe you—you of little faith? 31 So do not worry, saying, 'What shall we eat?' or 'What shall we drink?' or 'What shall we wear?' 32 For the pagans run after all these things, and your heavenly Father knows that you need them. 33 But seek first his kingdom and his righteousness, and all these things will be given to you as well. 34 Therefore do not worry about tomorrow, for tomorrow will worry about itself. Each day has enough trouble of its own. Matthew 6: 25-34

I should mention here that I was not raised to memorize Bible verses or to even know scripture. In many ways, God whispered to me to let my worries go. I felt in my heart that everything would be ok—that Arnoldo would be healed—that we would not lack in food or want for anything. Yet, the anxiety of it all got the best of me, and I would worry. I would feel the pit of my stomach double up in knots as I wrote out multiple checks every month. I've always been a *doer* type person—a *think outside of the box type*. So, my mind was always racing with ideas, with research I had read about his injury, with thoughts about what could help him. The overwhelming amount of information was a cause for anxiety and ultimately the unknowns were a cause of anxiety too. Had the doctors given up? He wasn't supposed to live—he wasn't supposed to wake up let alone ever talk or walk. For them, any *lack* of progress was expected. It confirmed the grimness of his prognosis. The steady strides he made were beyond their scope of understanding. The man was alive. That alone was unexplainable. I could not turn to them for help because their limited understanding of Arnoldo's condition was to expect the worst and be grateful for improvements. The doctors were so cautious about giving false hope. But what is *false hope?* Hope cannot be false. By its very nature—hope is the expectation of a positive outcome. It is the full expectation of healing for Arnoldo. To say that this is false is to live without faith. It is to believe that human understanding is greater than God. The very strength of hope is faith. Faith that God can do what is impossible for humans to comprehend. It was at this time I realized that I too was being driven by my own understanding. I realized that I was NOT fully relying on God. God was asking me to trust in him and here I was trying to take control—trying to fix everything. This was not up to me to fix. This was a journey about trust and faith—hope and healing.

I sat in the parking lot of my son's preschool. All the kids had been dropped off and I was not eager to go home. My heart was pounding in my chest. I could feel the voices in my head overpowering my physical body. *You need to be with your husband. You should have done... you shouldn't have... What are you going to do? What...?*

"Enough!" I screamed. "God help me—I can't do this alone." I felt angry, forsaken, abandoned. The cell phone in my purse began to ring. It was Sister Belinda, the nun in our parish. She had been leaving messages for the past few days, and I was so deep in my own worries and anxiety that I could not answer. Something told me to answer and I reached down to grab my phone.

"Hi, Sister B, how are you? Look, about Matthew—I just think it's too hard for me to get him to classes; we may have to postpone and do his first communion next year."

"Gabby, it's ok. We can figure out a way to get him to class, but that's not what I'm calling you about."

"Oh." I was silent for a moment; not sure why else she would call.

"A parishioner in our church, who wishes to remain anonymous, has donated to your family. The donation is for five thousand dollars." I was quiet—then I cleared my throat, choking back sobs.

"What? But how?"

"We were discussing your family and your situation, and how you are alone with the three boys, and how you have so much on your plate and so many expenses. This person wants to help." I was floored. God was showing me that HE was at work. I immediately thought of the treatment for Arnoldo. Five thousand dollars was more than half for one of the treatments. I could figure out the rest. *Thank you, God!* I came home with a light heart. I had another voicemail on my phone. It was the doctor—the one that was the head of the research team for the treatment. I dialed his number.

"Hi, Gabby, I know we discussed this treatment and I wanted to tell you that after really thinking about it—I want to give you a discounted rate. I can't charge you the nine thousand dollars. I can do them for five thousand per treatment." It was exactly what the person had donated. Exactly enough. God had answered prayers. Two days later, I got a phone call from a close friend.

"I have an envelope for you. Someone left it on my doorstep addressed to you."

"What? Why? Who was it?"

"I have no idea. It was anonymous." Later that day, we met at a park, and she handed me the envelope. It was sealed and my name was written on the front. Inside was a card with a beautifully hand-written note sending love and prayers to our family. Another small envelope was inside filled with five thousand dollars' worth of cashier's checks. I was speechless. Here was the payment for another treatment. In less than a week, God had shown me what he could do with faith and prayer. God was in control, and I simply had to trust.

I'm not going to go into detail about the treatments, but I can say this… we did see a marked improvement in Arnoldo's health. He was not completely healed, but he was definitely in less pain. I know God will do the rest.

Another miracle happened in November 2017, right before Arnoldo was hospitalized. At that point, Arnoldo had been home for several months, and I was feeling bone tired. The caregivers were tired, and my entire spirit was low. November also happens to be my birthday month, and it usually is the beginning of the holiday season for our family—my birthday, Thanksgiving, Arnoldo's birthday, Christmas, our anniversary, New Year's, Noah's birthday, Nico's birthday. A lot happening during this time of year. I have to say that ever since I have known Arnoldo, he has always done my birthday up in style. So much so, that every year he tried to think of ways to outdo himself from the previous year. He's done spa days with catered lunches, trips to the city with expensive purses and massages and French dinners, Nordstrom shopping sprees with a personal shopper, a limo wine tour with friends, expensive jewelry... but my most favorite gifts are books. He has filled my life with different books that he chooses, and it's so fun to look forward to his gifts.

This year I knew would be completely different. The spasms were getting worse, and the thought of starting the holiday season with him as sick as he was hurt my heart more than I could ever imagine. The spirit of heaviness dwelled in our home and around me. One evening, after dinner we were laying in bed and my heart was heavy. Arnoldo's body was stiffening, his nights had worsened, he had not spoken since July of that year and I felt fear in my heart. I felt fear of change, fear of the unknown. As I lay next to him, I whispered, *"What are we going to do..."* and sighed. It was more to myself than to him. I could hear him cough to clear his throat. This was common, as his swallowing was starting to become more and more difficult. He squeezed my hand and lifted his head.

"Have faith," he said. I sat up and stared at him. "Arnoldo, did you speak? Did you just say *have faith?*"

"Yes," he answered, his eyes overflowing with tears. I was overjoyed. "Mom, mom!" I yelled, calling for someone—anyone. I wanted to make sure I wasn't crazy. I wanted them to hear him speak too. My mother and aunt came running in, followed by the caregiver.

"He's talking! Arnoldo, can you say hi?"

"Hi," he said slowly.

"Arnoldo, you are talking! That is wonderful!" My mom's eyes were full of emotion.

"Yes," he answered.

"Hey, Arnoldo, you can talk." It was the caregiver.

"Hey," he answered. We were all shocked and thrilled that he was talking. But within a few moments, he cleared his throat and did not say a single word again. It is through these miraculous signs that I am able to continue this walk of faith. God spoke through him again. I know this to be true with all my heart and soul. Why? Because Arnoldo could have chosen to say so many things—*I love you. Hey, beautiful. Hey, sweetie. Hi, babe.* Instead, he said *have faith.* This was God. God also allowed there to be witnesses to this. The message was for me, but Arnoldo continued to speak in front of my mom, aunt, and the caregiver. It lasted for only a few moments, but it was enough. It was enough to give me the strength to carry on. I'll never forget the look of surprise on Arnoldo's face when he spoke. He clearly was just as surprised as I was. It would be another eleven months before we would hear his beautiful voice again.

October 12, 2018

We were at the hospital. The children and I held hands in a circle with Arnoldo and prayed for our little family. I led the prayer. I ended it by saying, "In Jesus' name, Amen." Arnoldo immediately said, "In Jesus' name, Amen." We all looked over at him in surprise.

"Dada, you talked!" exclaimed Matthew. Noah was beaming from ear to ear. Nico looked surprised. When we asked Arnoldo again if he realized that he spoke, he burst into tears. To date, he hasn't spoken again. However, every so often, Nico will remind me about this miracle.

Mommy, do you remember when Dada said Amen? Do you remember when Dada talked? I feel in my heart that it is God's way of reminding me to have FAITH. More miracles are on their way!

As of today, it has been nineteen months since Arnoldo suffered his brain injury. We have walked a path that I could have never imagined. It has been filled with ups and downs, fears, darkness, but also love, faith, and light. The person I am today is not the same person that lived on April 8, 2017. That woman did not know God the way I know him now. She had never been forced to cling to him as the storm surged around her.

One day, during my long drive to the hospital, it came to me that if I was given the chance to take this all back—to go back to the life we lived before, that I would *not* take that option. It is hard to imagine anyone saying that—especially with the pain and fear that filled the storm, and the anguish at watching the love of my life suffer day after day—yet, I know that the old Gabby did not know God the way he intended for her and for *all* of us to know him. The old Gabby was grateful but always wanted more. She was more in *this* world than in her promised life. The knowledge and understanding of suffering and loss was not with me. I now have God-given wisdom to offer others who are going through their own storm. Through pain, I have been strengthened. I have done things that I never imagined I could do, and that knowledge gives me strength. I pray and hope that God uses me as his ambassador here on earth to help so many others that are going through their own private pain and suffering.

The old Gabby was a daughter of God. This Gabby is not only his daughter, but also his warrior here on earth. There is no doubt in my mind of his existence—no doubt in my mind of his unconditional love, of his power, of his kingdom. The distractions of this world are our greatest enemy. They begin as seemingly harmless and benign, but they overpower the modern world. They keep us from prayer, from time alone with God, from fully hearing him. This is not an accident. Satan knows what and how to keep people—all people—from God. Yet, now that you have knowledge of this, you will know exactly how to defeat him. He doesn't win. That is the beauty in all of this. We know he loses;

it is just up to you to decide whether you choose to fight or sit it out. God is calling upon his warriors now. Ask yourself—has he called you? Sometimes, it is through the roughest storms that his call comes. Be prepared. Be still. Be ready to obey. The times in which we live require all of his people to put on the Armor of God. He wants ALL of us. Every single one. He loves YOU.

The power of this revelation was so great, and as I reflected on all this, I wondered if Arnoldo felt the same way. I wondered if this amazing human being, this loving husband and father and son and brother, who had suffered so much and continues to suffer, would feel that he too would not take any of this back if given the chance. My suffering had been emotional, but his was *both*. He was trapped in a body that did not work—that could not do what he knew he was meant to do, and he had to sit by and watch as his wife and boys ventured out in this storm alone. In addition, his condition was physically painful. The dystonia is excruciating and affected him from head to toes. He is barely able to scream, and he is forced to depend on others day in and day out. How could Arnoldo feel the same as I do? It is natural for him to wish it all away. Yet, as I meditated on this, I felt God urge me to ask him the question.

That morning when I arrived at the hospital, Arnoldo was laying in bed covered in sweat. I asked him to squeeze my hand if he was in pain. He wasn't. I went down the list—Thirsty? Itchy? Needing to be changed? He gave me a hard squeeze for needing to be changed. The nurses came in and worked on him. I stepped back and waited for them to be finished. When they left, he was comfortably laying on the bed. I asked him the question that was on my mind.

"Hey, babe, I have a question for you. I've been reflecting on this journey of ours—the ups and downs and pain of it all. If God came to you and said that, with one word, he could make everything go back to the way things were—go back to our old life on April 8th, the day before the accident —squeeze my hand if yes, you would choose to go back." I fully expected a hard squeeze, but there was none. I asked again. "If knowing what you know now, you would STILL continue down this same path that we are on, squeeze my..." He squeezed hard before I finished my sentence. "Arnoldo, this path? This path of illness and pain and hardship? If given the chance for all of this to go away, you would NOT choose for it to go away?" He squeezed again. I had tears running down my cheeks. I wanted to be sure. "Arnoldo, *only* squeeze my hand if you would still choose to be sick." He squeezed. "Is it because of our walk with God?" He squeezed harder. "Is it because it has brought you closer to God? He squeezed. "Is it because it has brought our family to God?" He squeezed again. "Is it because of this book? Because of the hope that it will help others?" He squeezed and sat up straighter in his bed. Tears streamed down his cheeks. Arnoldo too would not take this path back if given the chance. He too understood the sacredness of our walk with the Lord and the possibility of helping others. It certainly wasn't easy. Our lives would be forever changed, but we both live in the hope that we can help others find their own path of love and light in the storm.

This path has been dark and perilous, but God has never left us—*just as he has never left you.* We have learned to *be strong, to have faith, and to KNOW that everything will be ok.* This lesson we have learned intimately by our walk with God. I share it with you now because it is a lesson meant for all of mankind. *Believe. Stand Tall. Put on your armor every day and fight.* Today, we face many unknowns in the world. But focus on what you *do know.* Know God. Know that Jesus Christ is with you every second of every day. When you need him the most, he is carrying you through the storm. I am tired of seeing the love of my life suffer, and there is an ache in my heart for him to return home. Yet, I stand firm in *FAITH.* My Prayer of Power is for God to heal Arnoldo and bring him back to his family. I pray that together as one family we can change the world. Join Us. #PrayerofPower #PowerofPrayer

EPILOGUE

When Arnoldo had the cardiac arrest, that very first week, I had contacted a woman I knew in Hawaii that is a spiritual healer. Her very first words to me were *write this down*. I had felt those same words being whispered to me as I sat by his bedside in ICU, and I just could not even fathom writing down the pain and heartbreak that I was feeling. Later, as weeks turned into months, numerous other people would say those same words to me in different ways. *You should be writing this down. Have you thought about starting a blog? Gabby, I feel as though God is telling me to tell you to write this down. You could help so many people with your story. You guys need to tell your story. I see you and the kids and Arnoldo standing in front of congregations of people. He is healed. He is talking. You all are sharing your love. You are sharing messages of love with the world.*

The messages came one by one, over and over, and I stuffed them into the corners of my mind and ignored them. I focused on survival for him and for me and the kids. Yet, in the quiet moments of the night, I heard them whispered to me. When I finally heeded the call to write, it had been several months, and I had already written several letters to Arnoldo and the children. I started with those letters and went from there and kept writing. I figured that maybe when Arnoldo got better, he would want to read about the journey we had all been on. However, I kept hearing over and over that this book was *not* just for us. I kept hearing that this book would be for others too. This made me nervous.

Our story was so personal. So painful. Before I went any further, I wanted to make sure that writing this book would be something Arnoldo would want. After all, this was more *his story* than it was mine.

Arnoldo is a very private person, someone that struggled with social media, with being in the limelight in any way. I knew in my heart that if Arnoldo did *not* want any of this published, I would not do it. I remember the day I approached Arnoldo about the book. He was at the rehabilitation hospital for the second time and was struggling with the intense pain of dystonia. In a quiet moment, I started sharing with him how I kept hearing God tell me to write, and how through others there were the constant continued messages to write. He sat quietly in his bed until I finished. "But I want you to know that if you do not want me to write or publish this, I completely understand. After all, maybe this book is meant to be just for us. Maybe it is to help us to heal privately, without sharing with others. What do you think?" He tried to move, and a spasm gripped his body.

When it was over, he sat up in bed, and I helped to straighten him. I put my hand in his. "Arnoldo, if you feel that this book is meant to be written..." He gripped my hand hard for yes, without letting me finish. "Do you feel that this book is meant to be published and shared?" A harder squeeze this time. "Do you feel that maybe this is why this happened? That this is meant to be?" He sat up in bed and squeezed my hand. "Ok. So just so I can be sure. If you are on board with this book, this time raise your hand." He raised his arm up to his chin. I wanted him to know how personal this book was going to be—how much detail I was going to share, how our love and pain and sorrow would be on display for everyone, so I read to him one of the letters I had written him. As I finished the letter, he burst into tears. "You see, this is what I'm talking about. It's very personal. This is what the world is going to read. Do you still want this to be published?" He squeezed my hand for yes, firmly. He was completely on board. As I wrote each section of the book, or found old letters to add, I would read them to him. Our days together were spent reading old letters, reminiscing about the past, and talking about the future. It was beautiful.

I have to say that writing this book was not easy. Emotionally, it was reliving every horrible moment that I just wanted to forget about. Physically, it was difficult too. I was driving to the hospital at least three times per week. The hospital is close to two hours away from our home and I would spend ten to twelve hours there with him when I was there. When I was not at the hospital, I was at home trying to figure out insurance issues, government benefits for Arnoldo, communication with doctors, and dealing with bills and the household. I had found a lawyer that had started to help us navigate some of the complicated waters of his benefits. I had also started studying for my real estate exam because I felt an immense pressure to start working. Our savings was running out, and I was afraid of losing the house. In addition to all of this, I had the three children to care for. I drove them to and from school and to their activities, did homework with them and had doctors' appointments, and cooked and cleaned. They were all so young and each one of them needed us so much. Not to mention that they had been through so much and were trying to navigate their own pain.

I was torn in so many directions. It was around this time that things in our house suddenly started to fall apart. There were multiple water leaks, appliances started breaking down, and there was just a feeling of chaos that surrounded us. As God guided me through the intensity of living day by day, I started to put off writing. I felt as though there were constant crises to attend to, and the book was put on the back burner. Arnoldo was also not well. He would go for a few days looking and feeling better, and then suddenly, the spasms would come back full force, and I would be on the phone with doctors trying to figure out ways to help him. During my prayers, I would cry out to God and ask him for help, and I would hear him answer to *finish the book. Finish.* I kept hearing this word. After hearing this answer during prayer one day, I became angry. *Finish the book? How? How can I? I am up at 6:30 and by the time I am*

213

done tucking the last boy into bed, and making their lunches, and checking HW folders and folding laundry, and preparing for the next day, I am bone tired. How can I do this? You ask too much of me! I was angry and frustrated and overwhelmed.

To my surprise, God answered me. His answer was very clear. *Daughter, I have been waking you up at 5 am every day. There are quiet hours in the morning that you can use to write.* I was floored. For the past several weeks, I *would* be woken up at exactly 5 am, my heart pounding. I would roll over, look at the clock, groan and go back to sleep. I didn't need to be up and awake until around 6:45. My first instinct, instead of being thankful that God was showing me *how* to complete his call, was of frustration. It was cold out, and 5 am was early. I pictured myself sitting at my desk, cold and shivering, and not feeling any desire or inspiration to write. *NO, I can't do that. It's too cold. I don't want to get out of bed...* was my reply. God replied by showing me an image. The image was of me, wrapped up in my fluffy lavender robe. I was laying in my bed, warm and propped up on pillows, with a notebook and a pen in my hand. He said, *"You can handwrite the book. Find a notebook and a pen, and place them by your bed, along with a Bible. Remove all social media apps from your phone, go to sleep by 9 pm, and be ready to write. Pray and read from the Bible before starting to write."* I removed all the apps, found a notebook and pen and placed them on my nightstand.

Every day, at 4:57 am, I would be awakened by an unseen force. My heart was pounding, I would turn on my light and pray. Then, I would read from the Bible and start writing. This went on for many weeks. I was writing. It was working. God had answered my desperate call for help. Several weeks later, I was not going to bed at 9 pm as I had been instructed. Instead, I would stay up a little bit later and later. When my 5 am wake-up call would come, I was tired. I often would say in my head, *just ten more minutes. I'll wake up in ten.* Ten would turn to fifteen and sometimes it would be 6 am when I finally would turn on my light. This went on for several days, and then one day, I woke up, my heart pounding, at exactly 3 am. I could not go back to sleep. So, what did I do? I wrote. After the third day of being awakened at 3 am, I said to God, *OK, OK, I got the message! I'll wake up at 5 am!* He stopped the 3 am wake-up calls, but I learned two things. One, God has a sense of humor, and two, he was determined to help me succeed, in spite of myself! I love him so much, and I love that he loves me!

Arnoldo has been involved with this book from the very beginning. It is his story as much as it is our story. There are aspects to this story that he did not want in this book. He did not want any of his extended family, or his experiences from his childhood mentioned in the book. I can only assume that he wants to protect them, and that perhaps, he will one day be writing a sequel to this book where he can talk in more detail about those things that are more personal to him. My dear cousin Nena one day said, "Part Two of this book will be his story, told from his perspective. He is going to have so much to say about all that he heard and experienced. He has been silent all this time, but when he speaks it will be profound."

Today, we are standing in faith that the day will come when Arnoldo and the boys and I will travel the world to speak about this experience and share our love story. Arnoldo will write Part Two of this book—I know it. Join us in our Prayer of Power. Join us as we change the world. Join us as God answers prayers that will move mountains.

ACKNOWLEDGMENT

First and foremost, we give thanks to our Father God who has never left us and has held us through this storm. I want to thank my incredible mom Lydia Gannon for being by my side and caring for my children. Also, I want to acknowledge those who have made the publication of this book possible. Thank you to the entire staff at Celebration Center Preschool, Gabriela Manciulea, Rose Marie Kent, Pat and Gordon Lyster, Erika Alverdi from The Vine Refuge and Roszien Lewis from Confessions Publishing. Thank you for your belief in our story and for making it possible to share with the world.

I also want to thank ALL those that read the story in its rough draft form and gave me the encouragement and strength to keep writing. Thank you Jordan Gannon, Tony Gannon, Rachel Brown, Eve Gallegos, Ashley Pylant, Gabriela Manciulea, Silky Sahnan-Chan, María Elena Kahapea, Melissa Vongtama, Shannon Bounds, Erika Alverdi, Kristi Sanchez, Celeste Angelich, Susanne Abad, and Annie Jung.

I thank the countless unnamed individuals for their many acts of kindness and love shown towards our family.

Finally, there is an entire community of people, our local Brentwood community, that have never forgotten about our family and have continued to help us through prayer and service each and every day. Your love has made this possible.

ABOUT THE AUTHOR

Gabriella Avila is a Warrior for God, writer and advocate. She holds a BA in Religious Studies and a BA In History from California State University, Chico. She also holds a Juris Doctorate from Santa Clara University, School of Law.

Gabriella loves spontaneous road trips, unique food, good books and silly jokes. She believes that love is always the answer. She looks for God's miracles in the everyday and is practicing to be STILL.

Gabriella currently lives in the San Francisco Bay Area along with her husband, three sons and two dogs.

Follow Gabriella's journey by visiting her website: www.prayerofpower.com or contact her via email: authorgabbya@gmail.com

MEET OUR FAMILY . . .

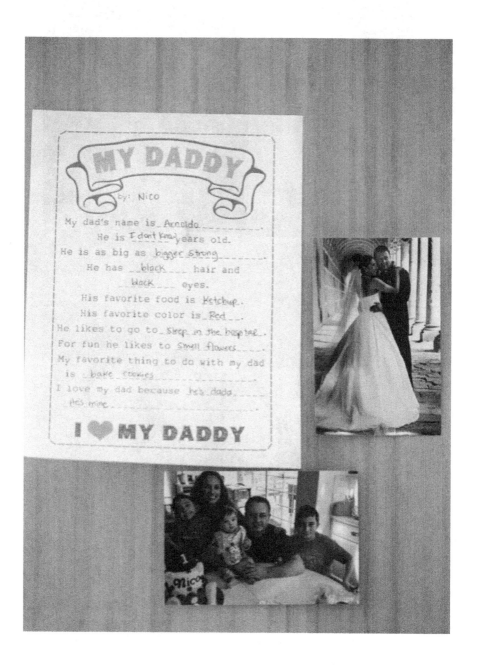

MY DADDY
by: Nico

My dad's name is Arnoldo.
He is I don't know years old.
He is as big as bigger strong.
He has black hair and
black eyes.
His favorite food is Ketchup.
His favorite color is Red.
He likes to go to sleep in the hospital.
For fun he likes to smell flowers.
My favorite thing to do with my dad
is bake cookies.
I love my dad because he's dada.
he's mine.

I ♥ MY DADDY

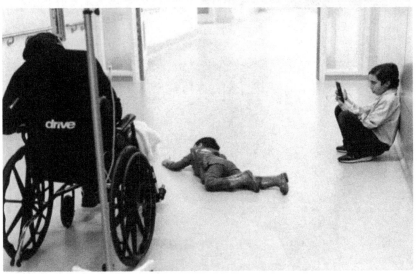

229

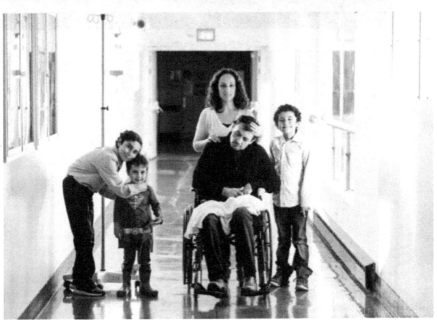

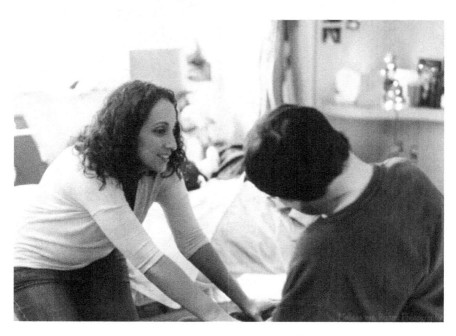

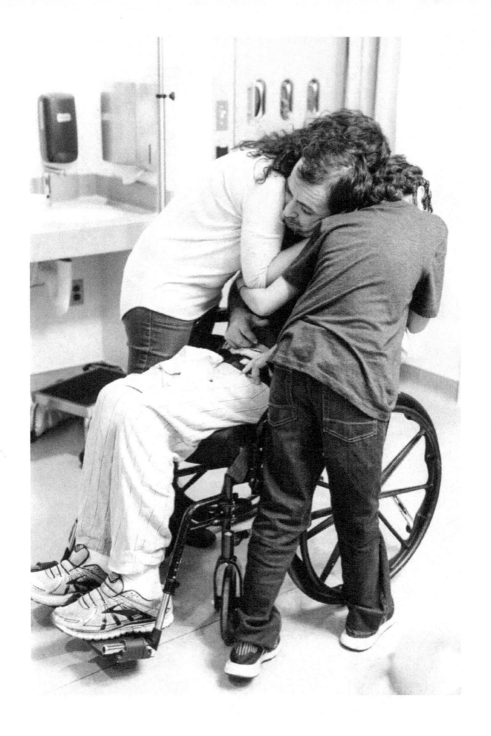

PRAYER
OF POWER . . .

Made in the
USA
Monee, IL